Elizabeth B. Mitchell

The Happy Town Planner

Miss E.B. Mitchell
by kind permission of St. George's School

Elizabeth B. Mitchell

The Happy Town Planner

Jean Lindsay

The Pentland Press Limited
Edinburgh · Cambridge · Durham

First published in 1993 by
The Pentland Press Ltd.
1 Hutton Close
South Church
Bishop Auckland
Durham

ISBN 1 85821 023 2

Typeset by Elite Typesetting Techniques, Southampton.
Printed and bound by Loader Jackson Printers

Dedicated
with permission
to
Professor Sir Robert Grieve

Acknowledgements

A great many people helped to produce this book. To thank them all would involve an enormous list. Charles Sleigh, former Secretary and Treasurer of St. George's School, put me in touch with Mrs Monteath, an old family friend of Miss Mitchell. She suggested that I should meet with Mrs Matilda Hall (neé Mitchell) a cousin of Miss Elizabeth. Mrs Hope and Mrs Sanderson brought Mrs Hall to meet me. Mrs Neill, the then Chairman of the St. George's School for Girls Old Girls' Association, agreed that a life of Miss Elizabeth should be produced. Mrs Rae told me of Brian Lambie of the Biggar Museum Trust who produced pictures, pamphlets and vivid recollections. He introduced me to the Rev. J. Warnock who provided invaluable material. Sir Robert Grieve read the MS, especially the parts about the town planning, and put me in touch with Mrs Edmonds who had worked with Miss Elizabeth in the Scottish section of the Town and Country Planning Association. The archivist of Miss Elizabeth's Oxford College has found most valuable information. Miss Garvin, the staff of the National Library and the staff of the Edinburgh Central Library have been indefatigable. The patience of the typists who retyped and retyped amended versions has been unbelievable. The staff of the Pentland Press have been magnificent. I am very grateful to all of them.

The opinions are entirely the responsibility of Jean Lindsay.

Contents

Illustrations

Chapter 1

Early Impressions 1880 – 1913

Miss Elizabeth Buchanan Mitchell, who died on her hundredth birthday in July 1980, was a Scotswoman who achieved considerable distinction but whose name is hardly known except to people interested in town planning. It is difficult to bring her to life for people who never met her. 'Who can describe Jerusalem?' Who can make a unique person come alive? Fortunately her personality comes across very vividly from her writings. There are scraps of autobiography in her *The Plan that Pleased* though this is ostensibly about the new town of East Kilbride. In her regular contributions to the *Town and Country Planning* magazine her style is unmistakable. Her comments are delightful. Her book on Western Canada contains a vivid picture of a young woman, full of interest, alert, observant, modest, honest and witty. Even her little handbook for church discussion groups about agricultural conditions in Scotland is characteristic. Her choice of subject is not obvious and her comments on conditions were those of someone who knew the 1920 Report on Agriculture very well.

She was the third daughter in a family of five girls and one boy, the children of a lawyer, Andrew Mitchell, and his wife, Jane Fordyce, née Mirrlees, whom he married in 1875.

Miss Mitchell's father being an advocate, it was natural that he should settle in Edinburgh. When he married he set up house in 56 Northumberland Street where the family lived till 1882 when they moved to a larger house at 9 Doune Terrace. There they lived for twenty-five years until Mr. Mitchell was appointed Sheriff Substitute for Stirling and the family moved there.

Miss Mitchell had strong connections with the religious life of Scotland. Her paternal great grandfather, the Rev. John Mitchell, D.D., had been Minister of the Anti-burgher, later the United Secession church of Wellington in Glasgow, and his father, the Rev. Andrew Mitchell, had been the

Anti-burgher Minister in Beith for 46 years. Miss Mitchell's sympathies were with the United Presbyterian Church which had been formed in 1847 when the Relief Church had joined the United Secession Church. The various divisions within the Church of Scotland are very complicated.[1] Miss Mitchell did not often discuss religion, but the tradition in which she had been brought up stood for respect for the individual conscience and the right of all the people, not just the Minister and Elders, or even the General Assembly, to decide Church policy.

Miss Elizabeth's character resembled that of her father quite remarkably. Though born in New York, Andrew Mitchell was essentially Glaswegian, educated at Glasgow Academy and Glasgow University. He then spread his wings, going to Trinity College, Oxford where, in 1868, he took a first in Literae Humaniores and a second in Law and History. He then went to the University of Edinburgh and in 1870 was admitted to the Faculty of Advocates. But he was not in active practice as Counsel. Instead he acquired considerable legal experience as an Interim Sheriff Substitute in various parts of Scotland including Falkirk, Stirling, Dunfermline, Forfar, Aberdeen and Glasgow where he served for long periods. After he took up residence in Edinburgh he became increasingly interested in local government. In 1891 he was elected to the Town Council and, except for an interval of eighteen months, he served on it until his move to Stirling in 1906.

In 1903 he was elected a Bailie. As his daughter was to be afterwards, he took special interest in slum property and in the social welfare of the citizens. He was much interested in the Y.M.C.A. and as early as 1880 was one of the directors of this Association. He was also a zealous churchman and was conspicuous for his attachment to the principles of 'voluntaryism', thus keeping alive the seceding tradition of his grandfather and great grandfather. For many years he took an active part in the Synod of the U.P. Church. He was also an active supporter of the Liberal Party, especially in the County of Lanark where his father had acquired two farms near Biggar.

The fact that Miss Elizabeth was brought up in central Edinburgh had a profound effect on her ideas of what towns should look like. As she wrote afterwards in her partly autobiographical *The Plan that Pleased* she knew

> the broad pavements of Moray Place, under the great pillars. The Moray Place gardens were good in their way, lawns good for running about and playing French and English, but far more interesting were

9 Doune Terrace, Edinburgh
Taken by Antonia Reeve

the Doune Terrace gardens. For there you went through an ordinary sort of gate and along an ordinary path round a corner, and then suddenly you found at your feet daisied slopes plunging down adventurously through sunshine and shadow to the dark river. Far above the depths soared the high piers and spans of the Dean Bridge, low and secret by the river was the dear little temple of St. Bernard's Well. There were caves, too, of great mystery behind the shrubs and trees of the upper banks. They had a structural purpose, but we did not know that. They were queer and hidden and gave us a thrill.[2]

As a child Miss Elizabeth did not realise that the gardens had not happened by themselves, that someone must have planned

the nooks so artfully using the contours of the ground, their belts of shrubbery so full of design to break the winds tearing along the ravine, their varied sunshine and shade. There had been, long ago, artists to create and a public to appreciate and pay for that dignified beauty between the Dean Bridge and Stockbridge. Contrast the thistley no man's land upstream on the same river below Coltbridge.[3]

But later when she came to consider town planning she realised what had been done to produce the places she had so much enjoyed.

These experiences gave Miss Elizabeth food for thought. The country just over the Dean Bridge and the friendly cottage at the top of Orchard Brae, where sometimes it was possible to buy pink rhubarb, were pleasant, but some streets were nasty. Even as a child she noticed that in Edinburgh, though streets were built with a very clear social distinction, there was no class separateness. Slummy Jamaica Street was at the back of elegant Heriot Row. The Nelsons lived beside their printing works among their workers. There was no remoteness as in Glasgow. Miss Elizabeth did not realise all this as a child but she was noticing things which she was to remember later.

All the girls went to St. George's School for Girls, Helen starting in 1888, the year when the school began, with the aim of providing good teaching by well qualified women to prepare girls for the university. Marian and Elizabeth joined her in 1891, Margaret in 1897 and Veronica in 1902. Before going to St. George's Elizabeth had been at Miss Murgham's School in Randolph Cliff for two years[4] but this was only a few minutes' walk further on. Later Miss Elizabeth was to lay much stress on being within walking distance of one's work.

The school was close to Doune Terrace and the children passed some of the most impressive examples of urban architecture on their journey there. They walked round Moray Place, along Great Stuart Street and Ainslie Place, round Randolph Crescent and across Queensferry Street and were at the school in Melville Street in about a quarter of an hour.

On leaving St. George's in 1898 Miss Mitchell applied for admission to Lady Margaret Hall, Oxford.[5] Pupils from St. George's had already gone to Cambridge but she was the first to go to Oxford. Perhaps she chose it because it had been her father's English university.

In those days Lady Margaret Hall was still only twenty years old and was just developing from a small, close-knit family into a properly constituted college though the atmosphere was still very like that of a private house: 'religious, intellectual, upper middle class and slightly old fashioned.'[6]

The Dean Bridge looking west along the Water of Leith and Doune Terrace Gardens
Taken by Antonia Reeve

St. George's School, Melville Street
by kind permission of St. George's School

Miss Elizabeth in VI form, 1898 (seated in second row, second from the right)
by kind permission of St. George's School

In her application form for Oxford Miss Mitchell said she had gone to Edinburgh University on leaving school, and she did not in fact take up her Oxford place till 1901. There is no record of her having graduated from Edinburgh and in *The Plan that Pleased* she says that her life in Edinburgh ended with a long illness during which she lay staring at the ceiling and after which she was sent to Italy to convalesce. Then she went to Lady Margaret Hall.

In a contribution to a symposium in honour of the Principal, Miss Mitchell described her arrival at the college. 'Coming as a stiff, shy, Scotch fresher to Gunfield I was embarrased to arrive with a Sunday hat and a bicycle, the rest of my luggage having stayed at Bletchley; Miss Wordsworth remained calm, lent me a very short nightdress and carried on with other things.'[7]

The Principal of LMH believed in girls living in small groups so that she, and other senior members of the college, could know them personally. Miss Mitchell with three other girls, Winifred Knox, Nellie Neild and Margaret Wickham, were in Gunfield, a house in which the Principal lived herself, in Norham Gardens next to the older Lady Margaret Hall buildings.[8]

Both Winifred Knox and Margaret Wickham were daughters of distinguished clergymen. The Rt. Rev. E.A. Knox was Bishop of Manchester and the Very Rev. Dr E.C. Wickham Dean of Lincoln. Winifred Knox was two years younger than Miss Mitchell and was the sister of Monseigneur Ronnie Knox. She took a first in History. Nellie Neild was a year younger than Miss Mitchell and also took a first in History, later winning the Alexander Medal of the Royal Historical Society and becoming a Headmistress. Margaret Wickham was the eldest of the group, being a year older than Miss Mitchell. She only got a second class in History and then trained for elementary school teaching and worked in Lincoln and India till 1922 after which she did voluntary work for the Oxford Mission.

Gunfield was a house which the Principal of LMH had tried to buy and, though the owner had refused, this lady left it in her will to the Principal who gave it to Lady Margaret Hall. The College Council leased it to the Principal so that Miss Mitchell and the other students saw a good deal of her. Miss Mitchell wrote later of her 'vast large heartedness'.

Examinations had not been open to women for very long but Miss Mitchell was the first Scots girl to achieve a double first in Classics, getting a First in Classical Moderations in 1904 and another, this time in the Final School of Literae Humaniores, in 1906. Miss Mitchell recorded very little about her time at Oxford but she did write some things about the Principal: 'Convention, generally speaking, did not exist for her, but a few she

Lady Margaret Hall. Miss Elizabeth is first on the left in the second row
by kind permission of Lady Margaret Hall

cherished like pets. We all ought to wear gloves and otherwise look tidy
within reason for it made a better impression on the University. No student
could go on being solemn and self-important with Miss Wordsworth about.
Her freedom of spirit was the same whether she was talking to a Royal
Duchess or to her four new freshers – her ranging knowledge that would
quote Homer or an eighteenth century statesman, a Prophet or Jane Austen
in the course of a conversation as if we knew them just as well as she did
was exhilarating. Nobody can describe Miss Wordsworth but how glad we
were that we knew her.'[9] Winifred Knox, later Lady Peck, has left a more
detailed picture.[10]

Girls might not go to tea or lunch with an undergraduate unless they were
chaperoned. None of them might bicycle on Sunday. They had to be in by
10 o'clock unless they had been given special leave. They might not walk
across a college quad alone. These restrictions seem intolerable to girls of
the late twentieth century but in 1901 they seemed 'those of any well

ordered home of the period'.[11] What the students found exhilarating was their new freedom. They might miss lectures and there would be no rebuke. They might walk or shop with a friend without having to find a chaperone. They might have tea alone in their own rooms 'instead of the mild tyranny of appearing trim and punctual in the drawing room at five o'clock'.[12] They could ensure privacy simply by putting an engaged notice on their door.

There was the excitement of seeing famous men in the streets. There were great preachers and inspiring lecturers. Winifred Knox enjoyed the hockey and the river but she does not mention whether Miss Elizabeth did. One rather surprising comment is that 'with such a notable exception as . . . my fastidious scholarly friend, Elizabeth, we were not interested in social contacts in Oxford.[13] They developed a distaste for the shoddy and the second rate, for second hand creeds, third rate gossip and unbalanced causes. Most important of all, they learnt to come to some sort of terms with the social conditions of the day. They read Charles Booth, Rowntree, Bernard Shaw and Wells. They read of socialism as a practical, if personally unpalatable, solution to the poverty and misery most of them had seen in the large cities. Some of their comments on the world around them revealed their ignorance, as when Winifred concluded a discussion by saying, 'Why, of course, *everyone* is a Conservative; no one decent could be a Liberal.'[14] She happened to choose for her small audience the daughter of a prominent Liberal member of the Scottish bar and the grand daughter of Mr Gladstone.

When girls left Oxford, professional openings were very few. Teaching in a school or college was a career for which an Oxford degree was invaluable but the pay was not good. The beginnings of the County Histories gave a chance for a few people to do research. One old don acted as a talent scout for a publisher and through him Miss Winifred Knox found herself working for two or three years on the life of St. Louis. It was eventually published and won kind reviews but it brought in only £30. A great many LMH graduates went home where their mothers were glad to have someone to do the flowers and share the social duties and parties and where fathers assured their daughters that they were perfectly able to keep them though some grumbled that, having paid college fees for some years, they must now pay for a trousseau. But even these apparently idle young women usually found a great deal to do. It was a period of great voluntary philanthropic activity, and settlements, committees, societies and clubs all wanted well educated, reliable, voluntary workers. Winifred Knox noted that 'Elizabeth after standing twice for Parliament as a Liberal candidate, devoted herself to a

career of public service well known in Scotland'.[15] She herself married into
the Education Department of Scotland where her husband, Sir James Peck,
was Permanent Secretary.[16]

The young graduates of Lady Margaret Hall were rather young for their
age. They were not much interested in dress, nor had many of them learnt to
dance or how to display social accomplishments or demonstrate any
suggestion of sex appeal. Only a dozen years after Miss Elizabeth's
generation had graduated the Great War killed most of the young men who
might have become their husbands. Winifred was lucky. All her four
brothers survived the War and so did Miss Elizabeth's brother. Miss
Elizabeth made one friend, probably through the Knox family – Harold
Macmillan, the future Prime Minister. He was fourteen years younger than
Miss Elizabeth but they found each other congenial and are said to have
remained lifelong friends.

While she was at Oxford Miss Elizabeth, like many other students, had
visited the University Women's Settlement in Southwark and the Lady
Margaret Hall Settlement in Lambeth. She was still worried about the
people who lived in the mean, ugly streets. During her last year she lived
with Mrs Arnold Toynbee, the widow of the Arnold Toynbee commemorated by Toynbee Hall in Whitechapel. It was in this house that Miss
Elizabeth heard about the work being done by a law reporter, Ebenezer
Howard, who had written a book deploring the endless spread of London
with its rush-hour crowds and monotonous suburbs. He had advocated the
creation of new towns where people could live in pleasant surroundings near
enough to walk to work. He had managed to attract the support of such
wealthy business men as Sir William Lever of Port Sunlight and the
Quakers with their experience of Bournville. Land had been bought near
Hitchin with money collected by the Company organising the project. In
1903 a new town, Letchworth, had been begun, which was to be the first
garden city in England. Miss Elizabeth was very much attracted by the
idea.[17]

After Miss Elizabeth left Oxford in 1906 she worked for a time as a
Classical Lecturer at Royal Holloway College at Egham in Surrey. Her one
recorded comment on this experience was that she enjoyed seeing the hats
worn by the ladies on their way to Ascot.

In 1909 she left Holloway and set up a school in Hampshire, St. Hilary's,
Wintney Court, Winchfield with Miss Pechinet as her partner. This lady had
been a Senior French lecturer at Holloway. Miss Mitchell wrote cheerfully
to her Oxford College saying that she hoped soon to send up candidates for
admission but in 1912 the school closed and she reported that she expected
to spend the winter at home.

Andrew Mitchell, Sheriff Substitute of Stirling
by kind permission of W. Green, publishers of the Scots Law Times

[1] See Appendix 1.
[2] *The Plan that Pleased.*
[3] Ibid.
[4] Application Form for admission to Lady Margaret Hall, Oxford.
[5] Ibid.
[6] Georgina Bathiscombe. *Reluctant Pioneer*
[7] Contribution to a symposium in honour of Miss Wordsworth in the LMH *Brown Book* 1933
[8] Georgina Bathiscombe, op. cit.
[9] LMH *Brown Book* 1933
[10] Lady W. Peck, *A Little Learning.*
[11] Ibid.
[12] Ibid.
[13] Ibid.
[14] Ibid.
[15] Ibid.
[16] Ibid.
[17] In her book on Canada Miss Mitchell wrote a statement of her view on the inestimable value of Settlements, see p.21

Chapter 2

Western Canada 1913-14

In the spring of 1913 Miss Elizabeth had the chance to observe a new town in process of being created when she went to stay with her cousin, Miss Lilias Mitchell, a deaconess in the very new town of North Battleford, Saskatchewan. The town had only been started seven years before Miss Elizabeth's visit and water had reached it only two years before she did. When in 1967 she came to write her book about town planning, *The Plan that Pleased*, it was plain that North Battleford had impressed her very much and that what she had seen there influenced her work later in Scotland but at the time when on her return home in 1914 she wrote *West Canada before the War* she devoted comparatively little space to town planning and ranged over many other aspects of Canadian development.

She said herself[1] that she wrote because she had been able to see what life was really like in little new towns and in prairie farms. This was because she 'was on the visit as a private person, not as a representative of any society or propaganda or business interest'[2] so she was allowed to look at things for herself and did not have shown to her what her friends thought she ought to see. She even apologised for having criticised some Canadian institutions but said that it was impossible for a Scot to feel like an outsider in Canada and that it had never been a Scots custom to abstain from all criticism of brothers and sisters.

She wrote her book, a serious study of some 40,000 words, for which she had supplemented her observations by a good deal of study, as soon as she got home.[3] She meant it to be a study of the major problems confronting Canada, particularly the retreat of farmers from the land and the danger of Canadian cities following the development of slums which occurred in Great Britain and the USA as a result of the Industrial Revolution. The book was well received by the critics but, as it appeared at the outbreak of the Great War, it did not sell well. In 1980 the publishers, John Murray, decided to bring out a new edition to celebrate Miss Elizabeth's 100th birthday and they intended her to receive a copy on her birthday morning but this was the day she died.

The little town of North Battleford Miss Elizabeth said she found very like England except that all the men seemed to be in real estate and that their wives, though they might be well off, all did most of their own work, though they had plenty of time for a cheerful social life. Even the richest woman had only one servant. She thought the people looked healthier than in England and the approach to economic equality was the great charm of the prairie city. There was no illness or hopeless poverty and though there were social distinctions these were based on wealth and there was less difference between rich and poor than in England. The men went daily to their office. The family house was usually of three storeys, brick built, and free standing on a small piece of ground.

She noticed that before a town was begun the plan had been drawn up consisting of a gridiron with streets running north and south and avenues east and west. An average street was 66 feet wide. As she wrote afterwards:

> In Britain, in those days, 'new town' was almost an improper word, a shocking visionary idea but in . . . Western Canada new towns were going up by dozens and I had the chance of seeing the process actually going on.[4]

She did not like the rigidity of the grid plan and she regretted that there were no playgrounds for small children or gardens where old people could sit. She noticed in passing that a city needed a focal point and that many Canadian towns had no central space with municipal buildings or a market though she did not elaborate on this. But in 1967 when she wrote *The Plan that Pleased* the impression was obviously still vivid in her mind:

> Where was the market-place, or piazza, to unite the citizens? Where could you place a fine building so that it could be properly seen as the culmination of a vista along the street, like St. George's dome in Edinburgh? Every street went on and on till it expired in an indefinite end.[5]

In August, she went to stay in a farm on the prairie though this astonished and rather horrified her friends. Her drive into the country to reach the farm, which was only twelve miles away, was full of surprises. North

Views of North Battleford
from pamphlet published in North Battleford

Battleford was surrounded not by fields of wheat but by a ring about five miles wide of vacant land which had been bought up to be resold at a considerable profit to developers as the town grew. There was no contact between the town and country.

Businessmen were at the top of the tree and landowning was no recommendation. This was very different from England where the King and the Dukes were all landowners and anyone wanting to 'get into society' would buy a country estate.

The journey to find the farm where Miss Elizabeth was to stay took all day. The roads were gay with prairie roses and Michaelmas daisies. These, with the all-embracing sunshine, made a golden background. But there were no sign posts, no farms and no one in the fields to tell them the way. At last, after about eight miles, they saw two men working on a binder. One spoke English, but he was very hazy as to where the farm was that they were looking for. He waved an arm vaguely north-west and said it was 'somewhere over there, several miles back'. They tried starting across country but trails made an inextricable maze. They tried keeping to the road but there was no sign of the farm. At last they saw a red object and plunged towards it. It was only a barn but beyond it was a tiny one-roomed shack where the owner was at home eating his solitary supper. He was an English-speaking Canadian and led them to a commanding point from where he could explain how to reach the farm. It was less than a mile north-east. They struck across some prairie and some ploughed land, round some bushes and some little mounds, keeping the sun behind them and a little to the left and so eventually found the farm and a warm welcome and most welcome supper. They had gone about ten miles out of their way and during the whole day had seen only three men, one of whom spoke no English.

Miss Elizabeth reached the prairie farmhouse in August and it was in that month that the first frost might be expected. If the wheat was not fully ripe it could be ruined by this frost. But in spite of the cold the weather from August to December was beautiful with brilliant sunshine. The crops were harvested and threshed and the visit of the threshing team was one of the busiest times in the life of the farmer's wife. From the first frost to the great cold in January was the time for social occasions. There was plenty of dancing and many pleasant evenings. But in January when the snow fell the cold was intense. One country woman drove in to town during this weather and got a 'frost stroke' and died. The winters were desperately long and the farm people shut themselves up early and read; one family had read the whole of Dickens and Thackeray.

Miss Elizabeth was astonished to find how law-abiding life was on the prairies. There were accidents because men were incredibly careless handling guns but very little crime. Farmers, when they were leaving home for any time, would leave the door open and chopped wood beside the stove. If someone came and used the wood he would cut more to leave behind when he left. Women would drive through dark solitude without a thought of danger.

The people who had come out into the prairie were fighters but their enemies were Frost, Drought, Solitude and Poverty. One of their difficulties was that they were not part of a group all fighting together to wring a living out of the prairie. Virgin soil would yield good crops for three or four years but then the quality of the crop declined. In times of difficulty a Dane or American or Galician might be a kind neighbour but not the same as someone of the farmer's own dialect, religion and ways.

The houses Miss Elizabeth found attractive. Some were of sawn planks brought from a town, others were of logs; these latter she preferred.

> An unhandy man will build an untidy house (especially with logs) off the perpendicular and tending to collapse but a log house built by capable hands efficiently plastered is far the most beautiful dwelling in the west . . . The ends of the round beams supporting the roof make a natural ornament, and the individual arrangement and shape of the windows gives each house an expression of its own, like our old cottages.[6]

Log houses were also warmer than those of planks. 'I shall not forget my first log house. From the outside I thought it was a hen house or stable not being accustomed to the style; but inside how noble the vision was.'[7] What struck her after the rounded, brown beams was the absence of all fussy mixed unnecessary ornament.

She was interested to find that a visitor was expected to share in the housework, for prairie farms very seldom had a hired girl to help.

> One makes acquaintance much quicker in the kitchen over the dish tub or cake tin than sitting in a proper chair in a drawing room with folded hands wondering what to say next.[8]

She admitted that prairie life was tough and that people might be old fashioned but she found that children grew up neither forward nor rough nor excitable. She thought that the idea that prairie farmers were rough might be partly the result of superficial appearances. The prairie man shaved very irregularly, partly because the water was preposterously hard and partly because hot water was very difficult to get. He wore overalls because they were convenient for his work but the hired man in these clothes might carry on a conversation on philology with the farmer and the prairie men were very merciful to their beasts.

Miss Elizabeth's first country entertainment had been a Homemakers' Tea in a school before she started her visit to the farm. The hostess with whom she was staying in the town was one of the few town dwellers to have contacts with the country and had been invited to speak to the Homemakers. Miss Elizabeth noted that punctuality was anything within the hour. 'There is nothing to set the clocks by and drives are long. The school clock was half an hour fast and the Tea started nearly an hour and a half late.'[9] She was, though, very impressed by the women gathered in the school. 'There were fine faces . . . strong mouths and straight eyes and quiet foreheads as of those who had looked Fate in the face and had not been cowed.'[10] They were full of hospitality and kindness but Miss Elizabeth felt out of place. 'I felt myself a poor spinster from a smaller world, and I went and hid in a corner with the schoolmistress, who was a spinster too.'[11] She was very favourably impressed by the efficiency with which the business was carried through and a delegation was collected to attend a Homemaker Lunch at the University in Saskatoon. 'I went away not knowing which to admire most, the business gifts of the Canadian farmer's wife or the practicality of the University of Saskatchewan.'[12]

The position of women in Canada interested Miss Elizabeth very much. She was impressed by the extent to which the men and women living on the prairie relied on one another and treated each other as equals. Yet when the question of suffrage came up, the Canadian women in the west had very little to say. As one of them explained, they never thought about this subject. Farmers saw no reason why their wives should not have the vote. It astonished Miss Elizabeth that, though she had travelled endlessly in Pullmans, locals and mixed trains, though she '[had] waited on railway platforms . . . passed through hotel bars and dined in small country eating houses . . . never a word of bad language came to [her] ears.'[13] She thought perhaps that in the presence of a woman Westerners bridled their tongues.

Women in the towns she found more difficult to understand. They were excellent housewives and few had hired help. After ten years or so conditions had become less primitive and electricity and running water had given women more leisure. Girls she found often had jobs as stenographers, store clerks or teachers but they seemed to have short hours and plenty of time to have 'a real good time'. Grace of girlhood she found not very usual in the town and she noted, 'I have a violent insular prejudice against all girls (and boys) who chew gum.'[14] She thought that there might be jobs for girls from Britain, but recommended that an educated girl should not come to Canada seeking work unless she had enough money to keep herself for a few months and then, if necessary, to buy her ticket home. There were jobs for teachers but the salaries were not good and the top jobs went to men. Stenographers were needed, so were nurses, but there was not enough money to pay the latter. She noticed that there were very few women to do odd voluntary jobs, find employment for the immigrant girls, sit on school boards, teach foreigners English or visit hospitals and thought that if two middle aged sisters were to settle in a little frontier town they would soon find plenty of voluntary work, for there was a place for the professional maiden aunt.

Girls from comfortable homes might well come to keep house for a brother farming on the prairie. But she added the warning that the best preparation for this would be to work as a general servant for six months either in England or in Canada.

During her visit, Miss Elizabeth managed to see quite a lot of Canadian universities and schools. Educational building, she found, was Saskatchewan's one extravagence. Public schools – that is schools run by the Government – amazed her:

> the quiet spacious sunny classrooms, with their comfortable fitted desks, their yards and yards of blackboard, the wide bright corridors, the flowers, the window boxes, the beauty and permanence of the buildings.[15]

The University at Saskatoon had an air of real permanence. She was delighted to find that the Entrance Examination for the Arts courses included compulsory Latin and that a Rhodes Scholar had come back as Professor of Greek. Miss Elizabeth was amused to hear that it was considered that some Rhodes scholars came back with a terrible Oxford manner, but their friends hoped this would rub off in time and yet something special be left.

> Both Oxford influence and classics might seem out of place in the youngest of the provinces, but perhaps they are very much in their right place. For platonist Oxford has never been satisfied with the ideal of mere abstract study or of an art and culture for an exclusive coterie. She has never been able to keep her thoughts long off politics of church and state.[16]

Beyond the arts building with its lecture rooms she caught sight, as she tacked across the windy campus, of strange unacademic buildings, a gigantic barn and a great shed for agricultural machinery, for Agriculture was a most important faculty. The Agricultural College and Experimental Farm she thought splendid but she regretted that their graduates did not return to the prairie as farmers.

The primary schools in the prairie she found most interesting. The children enjoyed coming to school for it broke the monotony. But she found some of the material offered to them dull, though children would read avidly *A Child's Garden of Verses* or hide in a corner at home to gallop through *The Pilgrim's Progress*. She thought that children were just as willing as ever to read books that were worthwhile if they did not get hold of trash first. She deplored rubbishy books and the ordinary cinema show. She thought that:

> the very hardness, solitude of the prairie give Saskatchewan an oppor-
> tunity for building up a real, sound culture, neither fanciful nor
> fashionable nor book-wormish and towards this end, I wish something
> could be done about the 'Readers'.[17]

In each prairie school there was one teacher, often young and inex-perienced and she did not stay long for she got married and disappeared 'into the sandy soil'. She would have little trouble from Inspectors or School Boards and if she enjoyed working independently she would be happy. Often there was no other building in sight from the school and one young teacher arrived to find that there was nowhere for her to live. At last one farm two or three miles away offered to accept her as a lodger and to lend her a horse to ride to and from school, but she was a town girl and could not ride horseback. There was talk in some districts of grouping several schools together in one central building so that the children might have the stimulus of different teachers and the teachers the chance of exchanging ideas with colleagues. But Miss Elizabeth did not think that this was a good idea for it would involve the children travelling considerable distances and in winter they would arrive in no fit state to work.

The work of the Churches interested Miss Elizabeth very much, though at first she found it odd that Matins was sparsely attended while Evensong was full to overflowing and that young men came to church on their own whereas housewives tended to stay at home. She was pleased to see the way in which various churches worked together and how there were no sectarian differences within any one of the churches. The Roman Catholics she found were mostly French Canadians or Irish Americans while the priests were usually French. The Church of England surprised her when after a decanal meeting she heard the conversation was all about English problems and, looking round the room, she realised that all the clergy were Englishmen. In the Church of England she found dioceses tended to be organised on ecclesiastical lines whether High Church or Evangelical but both collaborated peacefully. She thought that the Church of England did a very good job in these provinces, sending students out into the prairies in the summer under the direction of a 'driver', but expecting them to return in the winter to college. The Presbyterians were all one church whose members were Canadians from Down East and immigrants from Scotland. This church, she found, had taken an interest in the Ruthenians though at home in the Carpathians 'they seem[ed] generally to belong to a Uniate body, in communion with Rome but with rites like those of the Orthodox Church.'[18] Of the Methodists she saw comparatively little.

One feature of the religious life of Canada which Miss Elizabeth noted with some pleasure was the absence of 'new' religions. The Mormons had come in from the States and the Duokhobors from Russia but there was no Canadian Mrs Eddy.

There was little time for philanthropy. Money, when it was collected, was usually given to a church and if people needed help they were sent to the church. Organisations such as the Knights of Columbus or the Knights of Pythias were largely social. In the Church of England the women auxiliaries did a variety of good work. The Daughters of the Empire was the only society that Miss Elizabeth encountered that encouraged studious activities among its members. The Y.M.C.A. had now established an excellent club and the Y.W.C.A. provided lodging for teachers, stenographers and manual workers. There seemed very little need for the total abstinence society. Miss Elizabeth found that women did not drink and that overall there was very little drunkenness. She noted that in the larger cities Town Planning Societies existed but that 'the propaganda had not reached the smaller places, where land is cheaper and action easier'.[19]

She noted with regret that:

> there is one institution with an incalculable influence in England and the States which is only beginning to be known in Canada . . . the settlement, where the more fortunate do not work among the poor outsiders, but go and live among them and attempt the hard task of seeing things from their side.[20]

She heard of no settlements in the western cities though they were beginning in Winnipeg and she heard of several in Montreal and Toronto, though some of these she thought might be rather missions than settlements in the strictest sense.

> The pure high doctrine of the settlement as we learned it in Oxford from friends of the first founders was not that the rich should go to be missionaries to the poor, teach them, not even that they should go with charitable help, but that they should go and make acquaintance with their fellow countrymen. Oxford was to learn as much from Bethnal Green as Bethnal Green from Oxford; and this doctrine has never been altogether forgotten. Except for this, trained, professional workers would be more desirable 'settlers' than young men and women fresh from the universities, intending to take up different professions and positions in public life. The former would work more efficiently, but the settlement was originally designed for the young men and the young women, to open their eyes; and so study of economics and social questions, in conjunction with personal familiarity with the neighbours forms an important part of settlement life in London. The result is not so immediate but it may be more revolutionary. This side of the settlement purpose does not seem to be widely realised as yet in Canada, though there are signs of it in the McGill University settlement in Montreal, and also in Winnipeg. The University of Toronto, I think, is arranging a course in sociology.[21]

The second problem which troubled Miss Elizabeth greatly was the gradual drift of people away from the prairies into the town. As she drove about she saw weed-grown, abandoned farms and heard people talk of farming for three years or so and then going in to town and selling the homestead 'to somebody'.

The farmers got very little help from the towns. Their interests were different. The town liked the tariff which increased the price of goods wanted by the farmer. Town businessmen were prepared to give farmers credit which eventually ruined them. Machinery salesmen persuaded farmers to buy more machinery than they needed and if any of it went out of order the nearest machinery repair shop might be a hundred miles away. Some farmers sold their produce as far away as the east rather than selling it in the nearest town. Most of the press ignored the farmers and so did the politicians. At a Conference in Ottawa in March 1914 there were three sections. The two on town problems attracted hundreds of people, but the one on farming only between thirty and thirty-five. At the official opening of a new Collegiate building in Saskatchewan the Lieutenant Governor of the Province had stressed the need for higher education for farmers but the Headmaster, when he read out a list of the careers in which his boys had risen, made no mention of farming whatsoever.

For the last twenty or thirty years the old provinces had shown a drift away from agriculture and now the new prairie provinces were showing a similar drift. The population of Saskatchewan had gone up by leaps and bounds but this did not apply to the farming population and especially not to that of the farmers from Britain.

If arable farming was failing to attract settlers they might prefer mixed farming. This was less monotonous than growing wheat.

> The pig falls mysteriously ill and has to be nursed, or a calf is born in a great frost and has to be coaxed to live, or a horse strays from its pasture over hill and dale, or the poultry get up a great excitement because they see a white pigeon and think it is a new kind of hawk.[22]

But though mixed farming might be less monotonous the grind was a great deal harder.

> Day in day out, in fine or foul weather, in health or in sickness, the cows *must* be driven from the pasture and milked, the train horses watered and fed, the poultry fed and shut up, the eggs gathered.[23]

The farmers found that money invested in a farm brought no return. After a day's work the farmer was too tired for a social life of clubs or sports or baseball. At first his wife might want to be driven to meet neighbours but eventually she gave up any interest in social life. Some prairie wives went mad from loneliness.

The second and longer part of Miss Elizabeth's book on Canada contained her reflections on what she had seen.

The towns worried her for they were showing signs of developing along the same lines as those in Britain and the USA had done during the Industrial Revolution. Canadians were shocked by the slums in the old country, by the poor physique of the people and by the violence of protest there. But she was doubtful if the new towns in Canada, which were growing even as she observed them, could avoid slums and extreme poverty. In the towns there was much wealth but they produced nothing. Coal was not worked in Saskatchewan and water power had not yet proved easily available.

Something had been done to avoid slums. Every city was planned before a single lot was sold. A Canadian family expected a four-room house in its own lot which a working man could buy for $2,000, $150 down and $25 a month with interest until the whole was paid off. Wages might be $1,200 a year in Winnipeg. But there were signs that all was not well. Men might be unemployed for the intensely cold months and have to rely on their wives' earnings. Bricklayers might work seven months and carpenters for eight. Wages might seem high but so were prices. If a man could not buy a house, rent might be anything from $25 a month upward.

The people too were different from the slum populations Miss Elizabeth had met at home. Canadian physique was better than the average in England and thus hospitals usually catered for young, healthy men who had been hurt in accidents. The average age of the population was relatively young, with most people in their twenties. Canadian women took more pride in their neat appearance than their opposite numbers in Britain.

Conditions were however different in the big towns of the east. After a visit there, Miss Elizabeth was asked on her return to the west if she had not been impressed by such imposing buildings. She agreed that she had seen some fine business premises and public buildings along the main streets, but she did not mention that a very short distance away she had seen streets very like those of a newish working class district in Britain. Elizabeth Street she thought was as depressing as anything in the East End of London or central Edinburgh. She only heard of the surveys of various cities because she was a delegate at a conference, and she never saw them on sale in any bookshops. There were districts where foreign immigrants congregated and where water was still to be installed. When it was installed the owners of the houses had to install and connect the plumbing but about 60% of the houses were so poorly built that this was impossible. It was not surprising that 50% of the typhoid cases came from this district. 669 families lived there and of these 374 owned their houses and 282 were tenants. Ten did not pay rent and for three of these, information was not available. In one block in a new town there lived 141 Ruthenians, 36 Slovaks, 19 Russians, 19 Poles, 11 Austrians, 6 Italians and 6 Bokowinians. 89 lodged with 16 families. 40 men were 'batching'. There were no bath tubs and no waterborne sanitation, with only 23 dry closets. Only 23 of the houses had water taps. Infant mortality was 238.9 per 1,000 births and every fourth child was stillborn or died before it was one year old. TB was increasing and there were more deaths from it than cases reported. Progress towards alleviation of these conditions was not helped by the fact that in Winnipeg only about one person in ten was a property owner and entitled to vote.[24]

In Toronto the process of slum making had already gone far. Medical officers tried to prosecute in cases of very bad housing conditions but there were not adequate bylaws under which they could act. On the whole people were too busy to find out the truth. The majority thought that there was no danger of slums developing because there was a Town Planning Society, though its advertising had hardly reached the west, and because the church sent deaconesses into the bad areas. 'The poor deaconesses would be surprised to know with what power they are credited against forces, which have swept in the past over many a Parish Church.'[25]

But one of the most serious problems in the prairie provinces, and indeed throughout Canada, was immigration. Miss Elizabeth had encountered the problems posed by the nature of immigration as soon as she reached Canada. She arrived in May 1913 which was a record period for immigration. 'Three liners escaped together out of the fog, chased by another ship up the S. Lawrence and poured their thousands in one day in the quays of Quebec'.[26] The following night the CPR station at Montreal 'was a babel of every European tongue with wafts of broad Glasgow, as it seemed born floating triumphant over all'.[27] When she talked to her friends about immigration she found uneasiness: 'Last year you could place any able bodied man in ten minutes after his arrival. This year there are genuine skilled workmen on the tramp'.[28]

People did not only come from Europe. In 1907-8 7,000 Japanese had come in, but this had been reduced by 1913 to 700. In 1900-1 there were seven Chinese immigrants; in 1912-13 7,445. Indians from the Asian subcontinent were not numerous but the total population of India was so huge that millions could emigrate without causing any problem at home. People of a civilisation outside Christendom made assimilation in a small town impossible, not to speak of colour differences. There was resentment that orientals would accept lower wages than the native Canadians and push them out of work.

> Perhaps the feature of the west that took one personally most by surprise was the enormous number of vaguely defined South Eastern Europeans, not only in self contained communities but everywhere.[29]

The most notable fact was the increase in Russians not otherwise specified. In 1910-11 there had been 6,000 which had broken all previous records; in 1911-12 there were 9,000, in 1912-13 18,000. 'It was as if a sluice had been opened'.[30] One group of 'Russians', the Galicians, were demanding schools where children could be taught in their own language and Miss Elizabeth thought that if schools were no longer to be the place where Canadian national feeling was aroused in children it would never take place anywhere else. From what she had seen in Saskatchewan and Alberta she was convinced that:

> the prairie provinces have as sound human material as is available in any part of the Empire. The prairie provinces have the people to found a sober minded, united, stable society broad based upon prosperous farming and escaping the extremes alike of riches and poverty. Could such a healthy society be successfully created in these days within the Empire, out of men of British tradition, it would be no mean Imperial contribution, for its special qualities would strengthen the Empire just where of late years a weakness has been seen to exist.[31]

[1] *West Canada Before the War.*
[2] Ibid.
[3] Among the books and articles she quoted are *The Oxford Survey of the British Empire, The Anglo-Canadian Year Book,* Miss Sykes' *A Home Help in Canada,* Mrs Bradley's *Canada,* in the Home University Library, The Rev. John McDougall's *Rural Life in Canada,* F. Beer's 'Working Men's Houses in Canada' *in Town and Country Planning,* and Social surveys of various cities produced by the Social Services Board, Toronto.
[4] *The Plan that Pleased.*
[5] *The Plan that Pleased.*
[6] *West Canada before the War.*
[7] Ibid.
[8] Ibid.
[9] Ibid.
[10] Ibid.
[11] Ibid.
[12] Ibid.
[13] Ibid.
[14] Ibid.
[15] Ibid
[16] Ibid.
[17] Ibid.
[18] Ibid.
[19] Ibid.
[20] Ibid.
[21] Ibid.
[22] Ibid.
[23] Ibid.
[24] Ibid..
[25] Ibid.
[26] Ibid.
[27] Ibid.
[28] Ibid.
[29] Ibid.
[30] Ibid.
[31] Ibid.

Chapter 3

Settling in Biggar 1916

When in 1914 Miss Elizabeth came back after her visit to Canada she went to the house in Stirling where her parents had lived since 1906 when her father had become Sheriff Substitute for Stirling, but in 1915 Mr Andrew Mitchell died and the family split up. Miss Marian, the eldest surviving daughter, decided to stay in Stirling in a house which on her death she left to Miss Elizabeth. Mrs Mitchell, Miss Elizabeth and the two younger daughters, Miss Margaret and Miss Veronica, moved to Biggar, to Langlees which Miss Elizabeth called 'a little property' which her grandfather had bought in 1863 on the advice of his younger brother W.G. Mitchell who was living at Carwood, north of Biggar.

The property had originally consisted of two farms, Langlees and Knock. Knock was eventually demolished and only one wall remained standing. It marked the edge of the tennis court where Miss Elizabeth and her sisters used to play. The present house of Langlees was built for Andrew Mitchell by George, later Sir George, Washington Browne in 1890–91.[1] Miss Elizabeth used sometimes to talk about being taken by her father to Biggar to see where the house was to be built.

There is no evidence to show why Andrew Mitchell chose George Washington Browne as his architect. Perhaps he liked the architect's design for Edinburgh Central Library on George IV Bridge, built in 1887. His skill in using a precipitous site at Belford Road rather like the one in Biggar was not visible till 1891 and his Hospital for Sick Children was not built till 1892 or his own very attractive house on Blackford Road till 1899 but he had done some work for the U.P. church in 1880 and 1886 and it may have been through U.P. friends that Mr Mitchell heard of him. In 1883 he had also produced a design for the new City Chambers in Glasgow which on sheer merit should have won the competition, but popular taste was not ready for his subtle and economical treatment of Renaissance detail.[2]

Langlees
by kind permission of Biggar Museum

Biggar is said to consider itself the capital of the upper ward of Lanarkshire[3] and it certainly has one of the most spacious high streets of any Scots market town. The road is wide and bordered on either side with well pruned trees. The shops and workshops and other buildings, built of good whinstone, are set well back. The earlier part of the town, also built largely of whinstone, developed on the south side of the road round South Back Street but eventually attractive suburbs, again of whinstone, began to appear on the other side of the High Street. The houses were perched on a steep bank with sloping gardens below them which made the entrance to the town from Carwood very attractive.

The land had belonged to the Fleming family who built Boghall Castle at the south end of the town. It was a Fleming who had been with Robert the Bruce when he had stabbed the Comyn in a church in Dumfries. At one time the castle was one of the largest in the south of Scotland and most of the Scottish monarchs stayed there while on hunting expeditions in the Borders. In 1440 Malcolm Fleming was executed when the Earl of Douglas was executed for abusing his powers, but in 1451 the King realised that Fleming had been wrongfully executed and as a compensation created

Biggar a Burgh of Barony.[4] Mary Fleming, the daughter of the owner of the Castle, was a playmate of Mary Queen of Scots and in 1561 she was Queen for a Day in an Epiphany celebration at Court. In 1747 the last male heir of the Flemings died and the estate passed to the Elphinstones but they never lived in the castle and it fell into ruins.

But by the time of the second Statistical Account in the mid-nineteenth century the author could report that few parishes had been improved so much since the First Statistical Account at the end of the eighteenth century.[5] In the eighteenth century there had been very severe frosts especially in low lying farms so that grain could be used for seed only once in four or five years, but during the nineteenth century the land was drained and the frosts almost entirely disappeared.

Biggarshields, an estate to the north-east, was bought by a Mr Stainton in 1806 and in the years 1817, 1818, 1819 and 1820 he reclaimed 600 acres, planted 165 trees, erected 18 miles of stone dykes and planted 15 miles of hedgerow. In 1830[6] the Elphinstones broke the entail and parcels of land were sold off. Also in 1830 a Mr Gray acquired Carwood, further west, and followed Mr Stainton's example by reclaiming 400 acres, building stone dykes and planting hedges.

One part of the reclamation of the land was to control inundations by the Biggar Burn. This rose north of the town and after it had flowed out of the town at the south end of the High Street it entered a vale about seven miles long between the Clyde and the Tweed. Normally Biggar water flowed into the Tweed but when there had been exceptionally heavy rains the Clyde emptied part of its water into the Biggar Burn. But this was eventually brought under control.

The population of Biggar grew from 1,098 in 1760 to 1,216 in 1801 and to 2,049 in 1851. In 1760 a congregation of the Burghers' branch of the Secession Church set up a church in one of the pends off the High Street and in 1780 a congregation of the Relief Church was also set up.[7] In 1831 there were 48 families belonging to the Burgher Church and 118 belonging to the Relief.

One indication of the increasing prosperity of the town was the number of banks that began to operate there: the Commercial Bank in 1833 followed by the Western Bank of Scotland in 1840. When the latter one closed in 1857 the Royal Bank of Scotland opened a branch in the High Street.[8] A branch of the National Bank of Scotland took over the former City of Glasgow office and built new premises in 1863.

Biggar, like the rest of Lanarkshire, benefited from the general improvement in agriculture with the increased number of Clydesdale horses needed

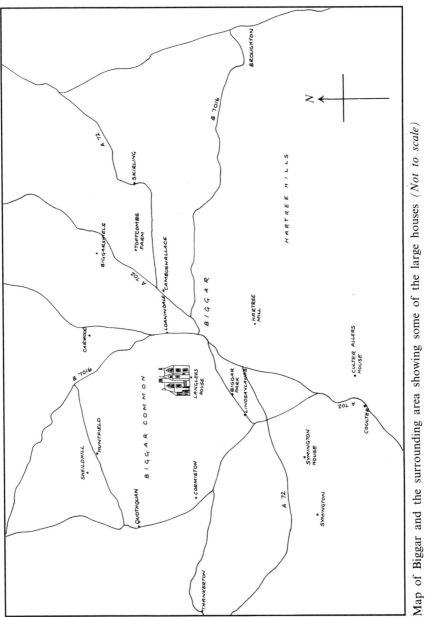

Map of Biggar and the surrounding area showing some of the large houses *(Not to scale)*

to work heavy ground and the introduction of Cheviot sheep and Ayrshire cattle. As an agricultural centre, Biggar had a large number of fairs taking place through the year:[9] in January a horse fair and hiring fair, in March a seed fair, in April and June two more horse fairs, in July a wool fair, in August a cattle fair and in September and October two more horse fairs. In 1874, however, an Auction Mart was set up and after that the number of fairs declined. Many animals were then sent to Lanark but Biggar remained the centre for selling sheep.

In 1839 a company set up a Gasworks.[10] In 1860 a Corn Exchange was built in the High Street to replace the delapidated and rat-infested Meal House. In 1885 piped water from Culter superseded water from local wells.[11] But the development which had most influence on the character of Biggar was the opening of the Symington, Biggar and Broughton railway in 1860.

Just how the arrival of the railway changed the life of Biggar can be understood when one reads of the connection between Biggar and other towns at the beginning of the nineteenth century. [12] The turnpike roads had improved towards the end of the eighteenth century [13] when, instead of local

Biggar Town Council
by kind permission of the Biggar Museum

men reluctantly repairing the roads, landowners contributed a sum which was used to pay for the work to be done efficiently. But even so traffic between towns was very limited. The coach between Edinburgh and Dumfries went through Biggar only every alternate day although the coach from Glasgow to Peebles went every day in summer and autumn. Carrier's carts went to Edinburgh three times a week and to Glasgow once a week. Carriers from Hawick to Glasgow and between Dumfries and Sanquhar went through Biggar once a week.[14]

Once this railway had been connected with the main line to Glasgow, gentlemen working in Glasgow could drive to the Biggar station, work in Glasgow and come home to be met by their coachman. In the summer gentlemen could spend part of their leisure in the country. Lady Peck[15], who had been to Oxford with Miss Elizabeth, mentions spending part of a holiday at Miss Elizabeth's home in the country.

One indication of the town's growing prosperity was the erection of a very impressive Burgher church at Moat Park in 1865 to replace the earlier one built off the High Street. One of the ministers of this earlier church had been the Rev. John Brown, father of the John Brown who wrote *Rab and his friends*.[16] In 1877 Gillespie Church was built in the High Street to replace the original Relief Church. Though the Burghers with the other sectors of the Secession Church had joined the Relief Church in 1847 to form the United Presbyterian church there was still a perceptible rivalry between the two churches. Moat Park attracted a rather more wealthy congregation, many of whom came a long way because there was no U.P. church near their home or because they admired the preaching at Moat Park.

One result of the decision of Lord Elphinstone to sell off parcels of land was the building of country mansions. At the end of the eighteenth century,[17] while Lord Elphistone was still the principal land holder, the land holder at Edmonston was the only heritor of any consideration. By the mid-nineteenth century,[18] though before the arrival of the railway, there were fifteen landowners, three of whom had estates worth more than £490 a year, as well as thirty-eight whose rents were worth less than £50 a year. Already a castellated mansion after a design by Gillespie Graham had been built near the old castle of Edmonston and a large mansion had been built in 1832 at Carwood. After the arrival of the railway[19] substantial buildings with extensive grounds were a prominent feature of the land surrounding Biggar. Outstanding buildings mentioned in the mid-twentieth century [20] were for the most part ones that had been mentioned a century earlier: Edmonston, Biggarshields, Biggar Park, Carwood, Cambus Wallace, Lindsaylands, though there were a few new ones such as Langlees and Loaningdale. Later in the twentieth century people who had lived in Biggar added[21] Huntfield, Coulter House, Cornhill, Hartree House, Comiston, Heavyside, Wyndales, Kirkwood and Quothquon Lodge.

The people living in these houses were retired colonial administrators such as James Cumming, or businessmen with Indian connections such as Victor Noel Paton, later Lord Ferrier. His house was once mistaken for a hotel when a complete stranger drove up and ordered a gin and tonic. Lord Ferrier brought two and sat down to drink his. The stranger asked in some surprise if this was not a hotel and Lord Ferrier then explained that it was his house.

Miss Ellen Dunlop, daughter of Sir Nathanial Dunlop who owned the Allan Line, lived at Shieldhill which now really is a hotel. Miss Galbraith lived at Lindsay Lands. There was Mr Collins, the Glasgow publisher. There were bankers like the Lorraines and Alex Stronach, who died when his bank failed. There was the Glasgow brewer James Neilson. There was McLellan, another Glasgow businessman involved in the production of Turkey red cloth and of rubber. The McCoshes of Gartsferry iron works had two houses in the district. Other residents included David Dickson, father of a doctor and an Edinburgh professor of Botany, whose family were friends of Sir Donald Tovey, and Murray of the Albion motor company. Some of the houses were let for the shooting and Sir Stephen Bilsland used to rent one. His daughter became the first Lady Clydesmuir. Sir Alexander Erskine Hill, Chairman of the 22 Committee was another of the local landowners.

It was a lively community. Since 1790 there had been a public library, another had been started in 1800 and a third, of exclusively theological works in 1807.[22] There was a long-established masonic lodge and a curling club which attracted enthusiastic support. In 1861 a Horticultural Society had been established which became a very busy part of Biggar life. Local landowners employed large numbers of gardeners, and whose flowers and fruit carried off the various prizes was of great importance. In addition to the flowers there were other entries such as home baking and later there was sometimes very hard feeling because a sponge cake which had been awarded first prize had certainly been made with the help of an electric beater.

There was also an Agricultural Show which attracted large numbers. There is a story that when Miss Elizabeth was at the show an entertainer who was begging and singing impromptu songs stopped behind her and sang:

> Lady over there, sitting on the grass
> She hasnae got a chair so she's sitting on her arse.

Monteath children at Biggar
by kind permission of Mrs Monteath Senior

There were one or two anxious glances in Miss Elizabeth's direction but she smiled broadly.

The Misses Mitchell, though they took an active part in the life of Biggar, supporting the Moat Park Church and the W.R.I. as well as the Flower Show and Agricultural Show and the triennial Moat Park Church Fete, and though they knew most of their neighbours, do not seem to have entertained very much. They were strict supporters of the temperance movement and rather than entertain their neighbours to dinner they preferred tea parties between about 3 and 5. There is a story about one of these tea parties when one of the local schoolmasters came to Langlees. During the course of the afternoon he mentioned that arthritis was making it very difficult for him to get up and down stairs. Miss Elizabeth promptly said that this was no problem and gathering her skirt about her she sat down and slid down the stairs.[23]

One group of visitors which was always welcome at Langlees was Miss Elizabeth's godaughter and her younger sister who was the godaughter of Miss Veronica. Another family which often visited Langlees was that of the

Doey and children
by kind permission of Mrs Monteath Senior

Andrew Monteath with Miss Elizabeth and Miss Veronica
by kind permission of Mrs Monteath Senior

Monteaths. Miss Elizabeth remembered Hester taking her first tottering steps before the admiring housekeeper Kate McMinn. The children remembered a particular tree with a big horizontal branch ideal for climbing. They also remembered special toys, one a sort of rickshaw in which one child could be pulled along by another.

In the early days at Langlees there was Doey. She had been an under-nursemaid and like so many nurses stayed on with the family long after the children had grown up. There is a delightful snap shot of Andrew Monteath aged four, sitting between Miss Elizabeth and Miss Veronica. From his very happy face there is no doubt that he enjoyed visiting Langlees very much indeed.[24]

[1] Information in a letter from Miss E.B. Mitchell to Brian Lambie 15 February 1952.
[2] A. Gomme and D. Walker, *Architecture of Glasgow.*
[3] Moray McLaren, *Shell Guide to Scotland.*
[4] W. Hunter, *Biggar and the House of Fleming.*
[5] Second Statistical Account.
[6] Ibid.
[7] Ibid.
[8] Ibid.
[9] Ordnance Gazeteer of Scotland 1891.
[10] David Littlejohn, *Biggar Town Trail.*
[11] Third Statistical Account gives date as 1850, but it was 1885.
[12] David Littlejohn, *Biggar Town Trail.*
[13] Second Statistical Account.
[14] First Statistical Account.

[15] Lady Winifred Peck, *A Little Learning.*
[16] David Littlejohn, *Biggar Town Trail.*
[17] First Statistical Account.
[18] Second Statistical Account.
[19] Third Statistical Account.
[20] Ibid.
[21] Verbal information from B. Lambie and Rev. J. Warnock.
[22] Second Statistical Account.
[23] Verbal information from one of the daughters of the visitor.
[24] Verbal information from Mrs Monteath, the mother of Hester and Andrew.

Chapter 4

Public Work in Lanarkshire

AGRICULTURE & WOMEN'S INSTITUTES 1917-18

At the beginning of the twentieth century, most young women of Miss Elizabeth's class with a private income did not expect to take up a paid profession. But Miss Elizabeth, like many of her contemporaries, felt the need to do some form of voluntary public work. The war made it easier for her to do this.

At the beginning of the war Miss Mitchell wrote to her Oxford College saying that she had been appointed a member and Honorary Secretary of the Scottish Committee on Women's Employment, the central body set up the previous autumn to advise on questions in connection with the National Relief Fund. She gave a list of some of the members of the committee and it was an impressive collection.[1]

> Shortly after moving to Biggar [Miss Mitchell] found [herself] engaged in the food production campaign, intensifying as the war went on towards those early months of 1917, with their appalling sinking of food ships. There was a Women's Agricultural Committee. [They] were trying to bring women from other occupations to the farms in an amateur experimental foreshadowing of the Women's Land Army during the Second World War. The Committee had a powerful chair-woman in Mrs Anne Douglas of Auchlonan, Lesmahagow, and another determined personality (more reserved) in Miss Ellen Dunlop of Shield-hill, Biggar.[2]

Miss Elizabeth was the honorary secretary.

Towards the end of the war a speaker from the Board of Agriculture for Scotland came to talk about Women's Institutes which were just starting in England. The Committee listened politely but non-committally until Miss

Elizabeth told them about what she had seen in Canada and how much
rural clubs for women had been valued in Saskatchewan and Alberta. The
Chairman of the Committee and another influential member went home to
see what, if anything, could be done in their parishes. The next month they
reported that each had started two clubs.

> Immediately after the war Mrs Douglas and [Miss Elizabeth] were
> together again as chairman and hon. secretary, respectively, of a
> committee officially appointed in 1919 to consider and report on the
> position of women in agriculture in Scotland.[3]

The Committees were an admirable preparation for Miss Mitchell's later
work in town planning. They

> interviewed many witnesses and went on tours of inquiry. Everywhere
> [their] main theme was the low standard of housing for farm-
> workers.[4]

Though Scotland was a small country, rural conditions varied considerably.
Miss Mitchell used the knowledge she had acquired on the Agricultural
Committee when she wrote a little book: *Agriculture in Scotland Today and
Tomorrow*. It was intended as a hand-book for Church discussion groups
but it gave a very vivid and complete picture of conditions in Scotland at the
end of the 1914-18 war.

The Committee heard evidence on a variety of subjects: rural housing; the
sort of work expected in different districts and in different farms; why farm
workers and especially ploughmen, tended to move very frequently so that
their wives always felt strangers and their children were perpetually changing schools; how much a farm worker could earn and how much he could
make from extra activities such as poultry keeping. They heard evidence not
only from the Lowlands but also from the Highlands where conditions were
very different. They heard about the Clearances and about Lord Lovat's
plans to plant trees in the Highlands to provide more work. They heard
about the 'black house' which Lord Lovat thought was worse than anything
west of Russia. They heard why Highland families built extensions to the
one house on their croft to evade the law limiting the building on a croft to
one house. They heard about the need for additional industries if the crofter
was to live in comfort. The problem of providing new industries or moving
old ones was something that interested Miss Elizabeth all her life. They
heard about the need for good rural education and why technical education
was essential if new industries were to be started in rural areas. The need for

such education for girls was stressed. One rather surprising topic brought to the notice of the Committee was the need to provide some social life for Lowland farm workers. Highlanders had their traditional ceilidhs with stories and jokes, songs and dances but the farm workers in the Lowlands had nothing comparable.

Perhaps rather to her surprise Miss Elizabeth found herself advocating a wide variety of activities in her handbook for Church discussion groups: Women's Rural Institutes, Farm Servants Unions, Co-operative Societies, Church Guilds, Musical Festivals, Dramatic Societies. She stressed the important part which could be played by the Church. As she had gone round taking evidence, she had been pleased to hear from a rural headmaster how glad he was that at last there was something for the women. The men had their markets and public houses, the children had their schools but the women had nothing.

LANARKSHIRE EDUCATION COMMITTEE 1919-29

Between 1919 and 1929 Miss Elizabeth served as an elected member of the Lanarkshire Education Authority. This body was elected by proportional representation and so tended to produce a steady central policy free of extremist views whether of left or right and it worked well in Lanarkshire till destroyed in 1929. The first three years on the Education Authority were particularly lively because it was taking over the work of some thirty parish school boards and many of the members of the Education Authority had been chairmen themselves. Gradually the members of the Education Authority learned to work together under the powerful control of old Sir Henry Keith of Hamilton. Miss Elizabeth had a great admiration for Sir Henry and said that if war or a strike or an earthquake had cut off Lanarkshire from London and Edinburgh, Sir Henry 'would step forward quite quietly and take charge'.[5]

In its brief span of life the authority had to its credit three principal achievements. It levelled up the extraordinary diversity of conditions between the parishes which had been bad in an educational sense and those which had been good; it did much to reduce overcrowding and to build up the staffs in the Roman Catholic schools . . . and in the building of schools Lanarkshire led a revolutionary change.[6]

In 1919 some of the school buildings were just shocking especially where there had been subsidence. White wash and chocolate paint were the

general rule; there might be a large photograph of the Lord Lieutenant
or of the Niagara Falls – just as might happen. The Roman Catholic
schools, on the other hand, though poor and grossly overcrowded, had
pictures; and I shall always remember old Father Dalbeke's tiny
garden.[7]

The Lanarkshire architect, John Stewart, was determined to make the
schools more attractive. His first new school was at Larkhill, a partly
mining village, good class as these villages went, but stoney and grey. From
the outside the school looked as grim as the village but inside it revealed
good lighting, bright colours and cheerful pictures. The grounds were
attractive too. John Stewart and the authority led the way towards amenity
in places where amenity had never been thought of.

Miss Elizabeth was not a member of the committee concerned specially
with school buildings but she was the convenor of the continuation classes
committee and this took her all over the county visiting evening schools.
The Depression which hit the world in the 30s

had fallen on Lanarkshire in the twenties. A great munitions district,
Lower Lanarkshire had been active at the highest pressure during the
war, drawing in manpower. Suddenly the war demand ceased; the
servicemen came home; and in the following year, the national
economic policies of Britain and the U.S.A. were cruelly hard on British
export industries . . . All Lanarkshire's heavy industries sank into
distress together, and the demobilized men stood in queues for 'the
dole'. Of all the tragedies, none was darker than that of the boys who
had left school and had no hope of a job. One of the day centres . . . was
in a derelict factory at Whifflet near Coatbridge, another in an old
condemned school in Motherwell, all cracked by subsidence from old
coal workings, with walls coming apart from the roof.[8]

Miss Elizabeth

had a good battle and happy success in obtaining a new building for the
Technical School at Coatbridge and . . . was concerned in the initiation
of the county circulating library.[9]

She wished that an artist had come to encourage the boys to cheer up the
walls with splashes of colour as had been done at a bright little settlement at
Belshill Cross. She always had amenities in mind.

ELECTIONEERING AND THE LIBERAL PARTY 1924-9

In 1924 and 1929 Miss Elizabeth stood as a Liberal Candidate for Parliament first for South Lanark and then in a by-election for North Lanark. She could hardly have chosen a worse time to stand as a Liberal. In the late nineteenth century the Party had been very strong in Scotland and Gladstone had attracted a great personal following. Even as late as 1918 the Liberals were still strong and gained 60 out of 74 Scottish seats but then the situation changed drastically. Lloyd George was criticised for being too generous to the Germans in the Peace negotiations at Versailles, and then his policy at home, when he was confronted by strikes, was also attacked. In Ireland the situation was explosive. Sinn Fein had won 73 seats in the General Election of 1918 but had refused to sit in Westminster and declared a Republic. A fourth Home Rule Bill failed to quieten the situation and it looked as if military force would have to be used. There was friction between Lloyd George and Asquith, and Lloyd George was even accused of bestowing honours in return for donations to the party funds. In this atmosphere the Conservatives grew stronger and so did the infant Labour Party. In 1922 Labour took 30 of the Scottish seats and by 1924 the Liberals held only 9. In 1929 the Liberals did slightly better, winning 14 seats but this did not match the Labour 38. It was no wonder that both times she stood for election Miss Elizabeth lost her deposit.

The districts in which she campaigned were semi-rural, ringed round with the densely populated constituencies of Rutherglen, Airdrie and Coatbridge, Bothwell, Motherwell and Wishaw, and Hamilton. Part of South Lanark was rural and part consisted of mining areas. North Lanark was chiefly made up of mining villages on a high, windy plateau, along with the populous neighbourhood of Bishopbriggs backing on Glasgow.[10]

Her electioneering took her to many different parts of the country. She saw how wretched was the housing in the mining villages:

There were many one-roomed houses, few or no pithead baths, often outside dry lavatories shared.[11]

The scenes were grim but the audiences were amiable even on a Friday night when a little drunk.[12]

She was much impressed, however, by the people:

There was an earnest kind of miner, especially in south Lanarkshire, very like the old covenanters in the same hillsides.[13]

From her electioneering campaigns

> two deep impressions remained – the fearful need both for better
> housing and for greater mobility of labour . . . Trade Union demarca-
> tion forbade a man passing from one occupation to another where he
> lived, and the housing situation made it almost impossible for a family
> man to move to another place since the new housing to relieve the cruel
> scarcity was in the hands of separate local authorities, each concerned
> for its own people.[14]

Incomers were hopelessly far down the list of applications for houses, and
overseas emigration, which had been an alternative possibility before 1913,
had become severely limited.

The electioneering was very briefly reported in the local press, the
Hamilton Advertiser. Miss Elizabeth's opponent in 1924, the Unionist
candidate, was another Mitchell, Stephen, who came from Stirlingshire and
was Managing Director of the two hundred-year-old tobacco firm of
Mitchell & Son, a branch of Imperial Tobacco. He had been educated at
Loretto School, Musselburgh and Jesus College, Cambridge. Polling Day
was apparently wet and cold, but the three candidates concluded their
campaigns by addressing crowded meetings. When the Unionist candidate's
victory was announced there were scenes of great animation and Mr
Mitchell was carried shoulder high to the market where about 2,000 people
were present.

The by-election of 1929 was rather more fully reported. In January the
ex-Provost was invited to address various prospective Liberal candidates
but it was not till the beginning of March that Miss Elizabeth, vice President
of the Scottish Liberal Federation, was adopted as the Liberal candidate
and she announced that she would fight the election on the unemployment
issue. When she opened her campaign she got a good reception from
crowded audiences. It was a triangular contest between Liberal, Unionist
and Labour and when the votes were counted the Labour Candidate, Jenny
Lee, got 15,711, the Unionist 9,133 and Miss Mitchell only 2,488 votes.
Although she lost her deposit the Liberals of North Lanark presented her
with a beautiful silver rose bowl and she was described as a splendid
candidate whose campaign had been exhilarating. Miss Mitchell in her
speech of thanks said how glad she was that the Association had stood so
loyally by her. She was convinced that the contest had dissipated the idea
that the Liberals were a small and depressed party acting as hewers of wood
and drawers of water for the Conservatives. She expressed pleasure that the
party, though it had decided not to contest the next election because it was

too soon after the by-election, was preparing to contest the election after that. The journalist noted that Miss Mitchell would be busy for she had agreed to speak at a great many meetings in support of Liberal causes.[15]

J.P. IN LANARK 1925 ONWARDS

Among her many other activities Miss Elizabeth also served as a J.P., sitting in Lanark where she had taken the oath in May 1925. In this connection some words from the obituary of her father in the *Scottish Law Review* 1915 might almost have been written about Miss Elizabeth herself.

> As a judge he was painstaking and conscientious to an extreme degree, doing his best to uphold the traditions of the bench. As a man of sterling character, he enjoyed the respect and esteem of a wide circle of friends.

Miss Elizabeth obviously took after her father.

The Justices of the Peace had been introduced into Scotland by James VI in 1587, confirmed in 1609 and again in 1617, 1633 and 1661. After the Union with England in 1707 an attempt was made to organise the Justices of the Peace on the same lines as the J.P.s in England but they never gained the same standing, partly because of the heredity jurisdiction enjoyed by some landholders, and partly because in the Burghs justice was administered by the Burgh Courts.

For two hundred years after 1767 justices of the Peace were appointed by the Lord Chancellor. The Justices sat in a County district for which they had been appointed. They usually sat three together but sometimes there were only two.

During the earlier part of the nineteenth century their administrative powers had been considerable. For a time they fixed rates of wages for workers and labourers but this was transferred to County Councils together with such various and varied other duties as the regulation of gas meters (under the Sale of Gas Act 1859), the regulation of weights and measures (under the Act of 1878), the appointment of asylum visitors (under the Lunacy Act (Scotland) 1859), the licensing of factories manufacturing explosives (under the Explosive Act of 1875), and the licensing of retreats for habitual drunkards (under the Inebriates Act of 1888). They had even been responsible for the protection of wild birds under Acts of 1880 and 1881, for licensing theatres under the Theatres Act of 1843, and licensing pawn brokers under an Act of 1872. They also granted licences for the sale of guns (under the Game Licence Act of 1860) and the licensing of Clubs which might sell intoxicating liquors. At one time they supervised the regulation of ferries and fares charged by them.

By the time Miss Mitchell joined the bench much of the work had been taken out of the hands of the J.P.s. They continued to deal with licensing whether of hotels, public houses or grocers' premises. They took affidavits and certified signatures and formal documents. Occasionally there were cases of assault, and until 1971 they also dealt with juvenile cases.

[1] Lady Margaret Hall *Brown Book* 1915.
[2] *The Plan that Pleased.*
[3] *Report of the Committee on Women in Agriculture in Scotland 1920.*
[4] *The Plan that Pleased.*
[5] Ibid.
[6] Ibid.
[7] Ibid.
[8] Ibid.
[9] Ibid.
[10] Ibid.
[11] Ibid.
[12] Ibid.
[13] Ibid.
[14] Ibid.
[15] *Hamilton Advertiser*, 11 May 1929.

Chapter 5

St. George's School

HON. SECRETARY TO THE COUNCIL 1917–51

In spite of her public work and involvement in the life of Biggar Miss Mitchell found time to work for her old school for thirty-four years as Hon. Secretary to the Council and after that for six years as full member of the Council.

In the special edition of the school magazine published to celebrate the school's jubilee in 1938 Miss Mitchell contributed an article on the Council. She remembered that when she first joined the school in 1891

> the Committee were Three. Olympian, remote, majestical, they sat at 'Break Up' on a narrow bench in the corner of the crowded gym. When Miss Houldsworth, serenely, and Miss Mair, magnificiently, had played their due parts in the ritual and when all the cheers for Committee, Miss Walker, Staff and the girls who were leaving had been given, Miss Urquhart brought down the house with 'Three Cheers for the girls who are staying.' At the School Party, gowned in black velvet and violet silk, the Committee received in a special room, and descended later to press turkey and trifle on their enraptured young guests. Is there any such awe and glory possible now in the youngest heart?[1]

Miss Mitchell noted that in addition to the Olympian Three, two other ladies had played a decisive part in the early days, though they were no longer actively present in 1891 – Miss Anne Dundas, who had provided Miss Walker's first salary as Head Mistress and Miss Robertson who had bought No. 3 Melville Street as the home of the new school.

> When I joined the Council, as Honorary Secretary in 1917, Miss Mair remained, and three others also continued the old tradition – Miss

Frances Simson of Masson Hall early added to the number, Miss Alice
Dowden, whom nobody could help loving, specially charged with the
care of the kitchen and household and Miss Walker who had passed
from Headmistress-ship to the Council. It is thanks to them and above
all to Miss Mair, that the Council has lingering about it still a nobler air
than is common in modern committees.[2]

Before this, in 1913 and 1914, the great change had been made. The private
venture of three brave ladies, who had risked so much for their educational
ideals, had become an incorporation with many contributors of capital; the
Murrayfield site had been bought, the new building constructed – only just
in time before the war; and the old Committee had become the larger and
more public Council. Lord Salveson became President of the Council at its
beginning in 1913 and, as Dame Sarah said, 'gave St. George's a place in his
heart second only to his beloved Zoo.' His special interest was in the
grounds and the outside of the school. 'When the flowering shrubs and trees
along the front of the field reach their full beauty, the generation of that day
will have Lord Salveson to thank.'[3]

St. George's School, Ravelston
by kind permission of St. George's School

During the war and afterwards the Council had a very anxious time . . . prices soared up, salaries of a fully qualified staff had to be raised, the surroundings, except the field, were chaos, the . . . courts grew black as a colliery, the Melville Street buildings were slow to sell . . . For years, finance was a constant anxiety and the most desirable improvements had to wait. Yet, when building began and progressed rapidly not far from the School, the Council were compelled to acquire the new field and the Braes and the railway field . . . Piggeries in the Braes haunted Mr Macpherson (the Treasurer). Bungalows in the lacrosse field would have been a disaster, and on the railway field a misfortune. The building of the studio and the science wing was another expense, well worthwhile but still adding to the expense.[4]

The history of the education provided by the school Miss Mitchell left to the Headmistress, but she concluded that

St. George's under Miss Aitken, in its spacious dwelling still holds by the ideals of learning and service set . . . by the Committee and Miss Walker, and through these years has won for itself a distinguished place and exercised a far reaching influence in the intellectual and social life of Scotland.[5]

This article was followed by a brief note from Mrs Hill Stewart, who had been a member of Council since 1913 and Chairman of the School Committee since 1931, giving a vivid picture of Miss Mitchell herself.

For fairly obvious reasons, no account of the work of the Honorary Secretary has been given in the preceding article. Miss Elizabeth Mitchell has acted as Honorary Secretary for 21 years [she was to continue in office as Secretary for another 13] and has been of invaluable service to the Council. Her clear, businesslike capacity, her foresight and her grasp of detail have guided it through many difficulties. Her charm of manner and her delightful personality have turned what might have been arduous toil into real pleasure. Beyond the ordinary routine work of a Secretary, Miss Mitchell has devoted herself to the development of the grounds and it is thanks to her energy and expert advice that they and the gardens of the Boarding House have been so well planned and cared for. (Even in the midst of the jubilee celebrations, Miss Mitchell was seen anxiously examining the roots of one of the 'Presentation Trees'.) May she long remain with us to prepare the Agenda, to write up the Minutes and to keep a watchful eye on the grounds.[6]

Miss Mitchell at St. George's Jubilee celebrations, 1938
by kind permission of St. George's School

Two of Miss Mitchell's contributions to the school grounds were not recorded in the Jubilee edition of the Chronicles. In 1931 at her instigation a special tree-planting ceremony was arranged, when trees were planted by Lord Salveson, Dame Sarah Mair, Miss Walker, Miss Frances Simson and Miss Alice Dowden. The trees chosen for Miss Simson and Miss Dowden were pink flowering cherries planted to the south of the school opposite the official front door. When, after the Second World War, a new Art Department was built, these trees had to be cut down, but were replaced by similar trees with little metal tags to show which ladies the new trees represented. The tree for Miss Walker is said to have been a white cherry. When four new classrooms, G1, G2, M1 and M2 were built this tree was cut down and thrown on a rubbish heap to burn, but the groundsman, Mr H. Gallacher, rescued it and replanted it outside Houldsworth boarding house. Certainly a rather lopsided white cherry was growing between the boarding house and the road in the 1960s.

In the same school year as the ceremonial planting of trees, Miss Mitchell wrote a letter to the school Chronicle asking girls who were leaving and wanted to give a present to the school to give trees or shrubs. She was able to tell them that a beginning had been made with little trees and holly hedges though as yet these were so small that girls were tempted to jump over them as Remus had jumped over the walls of Romulus' early Rome.

In 1932 Miss Mitchell reminded the Council that it had been the custom to do some special improvement to the grounds each year but by then the slump had begun to cause the school great anxiety.

Unfortunately there is no companion report by Miss Mitchell herself to cover her last years as Hon. Secretary to the Council from 1938-51. The main preoccupation was the effect of the war. Miss Mitchell said that she had been enormously impressed by the Headmistress, Miss Aitken's, preparation for evacuation. But the removal of numbers of girls to three different mansions in the Borders caused considerable problems. The school numbers fell and it was impossible to attract new girls. In April 1942 a subcommittee of Mrs Hill Stewart, the Head Mistress and Miss Mitchell advised that the school must return to Edinburgh or it might have to close. Corporation schools and three of the Merchant Companies schools were still functioning in Edinburgh. In fact, the school did return to the city but the move was extremely difficult for the school buildings and one boarding house had been taken over by the Army and the other boarding house was occupied by the Auxiliary Fire Service. Some classes were housed in the Headmistress's own house in Garscube Terrace, while other houses in this street were rented. Eventually, however, the Fire Service and the Army moved out, numbers began to pick up and it was possible to recruit more staff to replace those who had been made redundant because of falling numbers during the war. By the time Miss Mitchell approached the time when she was to retire from the Council in 1957, the school's finances had become far more steady and the Treasurer felt that at last he could take Miss Walker's legacy of £5,000 off deposit where he had kept it against an overdraft.

When Miss Mitchell decided to retire, the then President of the Council, Lord Keith, said he hoped there might be another tree planting ceremony so that she might be remembered by a tree of her choice. After she retired as Hon. Secretary Miss Mitchell served as Vice Chairman of the Council and when she resigned that office and moved to Stirling it must have given her satisfaction to see the school with long waiting lists and a very distinguished academic standard. Indeed, when there was to be an inspection after a new Headmistress had been appointed in 1960, the Scottish Department of Education had difficulty in finding enough Inspectors for so many of them had daughters at the school.

[1] *St. George's Jubilee Chronicle* 1938.
[2] Ibid.
[3] Ibid.
[4] Ibid.
[5] Ibid.
[6] Ibid.

Chapter 6

Involvement in Biggar 1935–1956

For the rest of her life Miss Elizabeth was much involved in the affairs of Biggar. From 1935-53 she was a member of the Town Council and a rather formidable one. She was never afraid to stand up for a policy which she believed was right, and she was apt to provide money for a scheme which might otherwise not have achieved success. In 1947 she was appointed Convener of the Housing Committee which gave her first-hand experience of housing problems. She was never elected Provost but this was characteristic of her. She was much more often to be found as the secretary of a group than as the chairman.

Two places in Biggar show Miss Elizabeth's interest in making a town attractive. One is next to a little group of houses put up by the local authority at the end of Lindsayland Road on the way to Langlees. Miss Mitchell insisted on planting a group of trees at the end of the little group. Some people thought this was a waste of money and that the trees would be destroyed, but she noted with satisfaction that the children liked playing in 'the planny and picking posies'[1] and the trees are very healthy and well grown today.

The other place in Biggar that shows Miss Elizabeth's enthusiasm for making places attractive is in the High Street on the north side just before the Cadger's Bridge. Facing the High Street is a handsome old stone house and behind it was a little triangle of land which seemed to be of no use. Miss Mitchell acquired the little triangle and gave it to the Council, stipulating that she would like to see homes built there for widows and single people. The Council called the little triangle Mitchell Knowe, which pleased Miss Elizabeth very much. She also restored the old house fronting the High Street. The place is now known as the Mitchell Knowe. Part of the old house Miss Elizabeth made available to Mrs Polanska, one of the very few Polish women who escaped to Britain. She thought that her husband had been killed and eventually married another Pole. Scotland was full of Polish soldiers at this time and Biggar had many of them. Mrs Polanska used to go up to Langlees to do light housework and help the housekeeper, Kate McMin, who had been with the family a long time. Everyone was very surprised when Mrs Polanska's first husband appeared. When Miss Elizabeth died she left to Mrs Polanska the part of the house which she had occupied. She also left the lower part of the house to the tradesman who had occupied it.

In 1975 Biggar Town Council ceased to exist when local government was reorganised.

Miss Elizabeth was deeply interested in the affairs of the local U.F. Churches. She was deeply religious and her religion was most practical. Conviction led to dedication and an unrelenting and passionate campaign of active service. She did not talk much, if at all, about her deep convictions but over the years she talked with her minister, the Rev. John Warnock. Her indignation at the blatant inequalities in Lanarkshire after 1918 was profound. God might not be in a hurry but she was. Her inner beliefs compelled her to action.[2]

In 1946, the Rev. John Warnock was inducted as minister of the Gillespie Moat Park Churches which had just been combined. He then met Miss Elizabeth for the first time as she organised behind the scenes. In 1948 there were local problems about which church buildings should be used for worship and which as a hall. Miss Elizabeth's experience and tact were invaluable, for having lived in Biggar for thirty years she knew the local issues and the local people. She was determined that Moat Park Church, where her family had worshipped, should be used for services and Gillespie as a hall. There was a good deal of feeling about this and Miss Elizabeth came in for some criticism from the members of Gillespie church, but her gentleness and sincerity and good judgement eventually weathered the storm. Unfortunately the floor of Moat Park Church fell in and the church had to be closed for repairs so that for a time Gillespie was used. In 1952 the refurbished Moat Park Church was reopened for worship but some people were tired of moving from one church to another and back again and made a final move to the parish church of St. Mary's which had celebrated its 400th anniversary in 1946, being the last collegiate church to be built in Scotland before the Reformation.

When Moat Park church was reopened for worship Miss Elizabeth had done much to smooth the way. She was a member of the Congregational Board and it was about this time that, though her activity in church affairs increased, she began to realise that, as she put it, 'I might suddenly disappear'. She began to arrange for other people to be trained to succeed her. In 1955 the Rev. J. Warnock was appointed Moderator of the Presbytery which involved travelling long distances in all sorts of weather, but thanks to the initiative of Miss E.B. Mitchell and other benefactors he was given a new motor car. In 1959 Mr Warnock celebrated twenty-five years in the Ministry and was presented with a new set of robes. Miss Elizabeth insisted that they should be of heavy silk, which proved very comfortable in winter but rather hot in summer. In 1961 the little parish of Elsrickle to the north of Biggar was linked with Gillespie Moat Park Church in Biggar which pleased Miss Mitchell because it had been another U.F. Church.

1951 was the 500th anniversary of Biggar being made a burgh of barony and it was proposed by Mr Lambie at the town council to have special celebrations. There was very little support for the idea but one of the two councillors who supported it was Miss Mitchell and things got done. One of the celebrations was to be a walking of the bounds, comparable to the annual activities at Galashiels, Peebles and Selkirk. There is an interesting letter from Miss Elizabeth to Mr Lambie about this function. She asked if he thought it would be a good idea to bring in a competent boy of the Senior Scout type when she, Mr Lambie and Mr Rae, the local poet, novelist and historian,[3] went to explore the route. She thought that each gentleman ought to have two boys for occasions that might arise. She went on to give her ideas about what the procession should be like. She thought that the procession should be led by a drummer and standard bearer and wondered if the needleworkers of the school could make a standard if one did not exist. If this had to be done she thought a grand permanent one should also be made. In fact, a standard was not ready for the 500th anniversary though a very splendid one is now in the Moat Park Museum care of the current Cornet. The next person, she thought, should be Mr Lambie, as the deputy chief of the Town Council, with his attendants following as nearly as possible the exact boundary. Then should come Mr Rae, the Chief, with his attendants, following the nearest convenient way. Then should come the people on foot, then ladies on palfreys and finally elders in cars. She mentioned to Mr Lambie that when they investigated the route, she might inspect Boghall as a Town Councillor as well as exploring the boundaries as a Warden of the Bounds. There is a delightful photograph of Miss Elizabeth taken on the exploratory walk on the Saturday before the procession.

The actual anniversary was on 31 March – a very wet cold day – but the boundaries were traced. Mr Lambie found himself involved in riding the

Walking the bounds of Biggar, 1951
photograph by Brian Lambie

bounds much against his will but he was one of the very few people on the Quincentary Anniversary Committee under sixty years old. Mr Lambie made two proclamations, one from the church door and one, in memory of William Wallace, at the Cadger's Bridge. In 1951 there were fifteen riders. (Nowadays this number has risen to a hundred but the riding takes place in June, not March, when the weather is more likely to be clement.) After the riding of the bounds there was a bonfire in the High Street. Glasgow University was celebrating its 500th anniversary at the same time and Walter Elliot, the Lord Rector of Glasgow, met the Provost of Biggar on the steps of St Mary's Church in Biggar to exchange congratulations.

On the evening before the riding of the bounds there was a dinner in the Corn Exchange when Sir Alex Douglas Home, who had been MP for some years, proposed the main toasts.

A year later, in February 1952, Miss Elizabeth was writing to Mr Lambie asking if he could sooner or later get hold of an old house that could be used for a town museum. She had noticed an old house at the top of the town with an interesting back, probably with a circular stair, but she admitted that she had never identified it from the front. She found the old cottages in Kirkstyle attractive and regretted that they were being closed one by one.

Then there were two old houses in Park Place, charming to look at but rather far down the town. The house she had bought for herself in the High Street was ideal for position but the inside had been so far gone that she had had to renew it completely. She feared that in a short time the oldest houses would all be condemned and pulled down 'and it would be nice if an interesting one could be picked out for love and preservation'.[4]

She was interested in seats where people could rest and asked Mr Lambie if he would think about a 'simple, strong, lasting seat' at Boghall with an inscription to the memory of Gilbert Rae, the poet who loved this local countryside. She admitted that she hoped an inscription might be put on the stone seat in Little Mitchellwood to the memory of Andrew and Jane Mitchell and their children but she realised that nothing could be done for the time being as four of the children were 'soldiering on'.[5]

She added in a P.S. that she felt that Mr Lambie was G. Rae's heir in taking an interest in such things.

Miss Elizabeth was always interested in Biggar buildings. In December 1956 she wrote to Mr Lambie forwarding a letter from Mr Lochhead asking various questions about old buildings. She was delighted to think that a list might be compiled of old buildings which might not be destroyed without at least serious consideration. She noted that Mr Lochhead was interested in

'Davaar', the old Parish Manse. She did not think it as old as most of the other buildings mentioned and wondered if it and the three old Kirkstyle cottages were the same date. She confessed that she had never been able to find the dates of Nos 47 and 51 but thought Davaar must be old as a number of the neighbouring houses paid feu duty to it. She noted that he had made no mention of the old house at the top of the town which Mr Lambie had liked the day they 'beat the bounds'.[6]

Gilbert Rae never got his seat and there is no inscription yet on the seat in Little Mitchellwood but there is a seat in memory of Miss Margaret Mitchell which is put out in the summer.

The list of old buildings compiled for the County council by the architect A.G. Lochhead, a friend of Miss Mitchell, formed the basis of the Listed Buildings. Biggar is now a Conservation Area.

---

[1] *The Plan that Pleased.*
[2] Typewritten notes by Rev. J. Warnock. Minister of Gillespie/Moat Park Church, Biggar 1946-1971.
[3] He was a local ironmonger with a profound interest in local history. He died in 1965.
[4] Miss E.B. Mitchell to Brian Lambie 15 February 1952.
[5] Miss E.B. Mitchell to Brian Lambie 20 January 1953.
[6] Miss E.B. Mitchell to Brian Lambie 4 December 1956.

Chapter 7

Town Planning: East Kilbride & Cumbernauld[1]

1937 – 1956 AND BEYOND

Miss E.B. Mitchell's chief preoccupation, which grew stronger from the '30s onwards, was with the creation of new towns to relieve the congestion of the Glasgow working class homes. In 1967 she told part of the story of her work in *The Plan that Pleased* and some more information can be found in the quarterly, later monthly, journal *Town and Country Planning*. In 1903, when Ebenezer Howard had founded Letchworth, a Garden Cities Association had been created which, after the Housing & Town Planning Act of 1909, changed its name to the Garden Cities and Town Planning Association. In 1941 the name was changed again to the Town and Country Planning Association.

For a long time Miss Mitchell had been interested in the ideas of Ebenezer Howard, and this interest increased when in 1920 he bought land near London and, supported by some of his friends from Letchworth, started a second garden city, Welwyn. Miss Mitchell said that one of her happiest recollections was that she had been one of the early shareholders in the Company responsible for the foundation of Welwyn. She used to visit the new Garden City from time to time to watch its progress and got to know both the Chairman of the Committee and the Manager. In 1926 Sir Ernest Simon started a similar garden city, Wythenshaw, outside Manchester.

From the 1930s onwards Miss Mitchell had more time to devote to the work of the Garden Cities and Town Planning Association. She was no longer convenor of the further education committee for Lanark and though she was still on the Education Committee it was only as a co-opted member and she had less to do. Her experience on the Biggar town council after 1935 showed her a little of town planning in action.

In spite of the Town & Country Planning Act of 1932 the '30s were a period when little house building was achieved. Except for housing built by unassisted private enterprise, 'progress' did not seem an appropriate word to describe the situation. Building by local authorities had declined and it was doubtful whether any of the houses built by private enterprise would help to solve the needs of the working classes.

In 1937, on the initiative of Gilbert McAllister, the Secretary of the Garden City and Town Planning Association, the few Scots members of the Association were called together in Glasgow and formed a Scottish branch.

Considering how large a part the Scottish Branch of the Town and Country Planning Association played in the creation of the new towns it is amazing how amateur it was. Mrs Edmonds, who was the Assistant Secretary from 1954 till Miss Mitchell retired in 1962, had vivid memories of the working of the Scottish Branch. It had no permanent office. Meetings of the Committee were held in the office of a member. Larger meetings with a speaker were held in premises rented for the occasion from a hotel or restaurant. The Secretary and Treasurer kept their own files. Much correspondence was sent to Miss Mitchell at her home and answered by her. Letters which had to be official and have copies kept were sent to the Assistant Secretary at her office as Depute Planning Officer of the Renfrew County Council which allowed the Town and Country Planning Association to have the documents typed. The Scottish Notes for the journal of the Town and Country Planning Association were written by Miss Mitchell and sent direct to London. The Assistant Secretary and Miss Mitchell wrote the Scottish Report for the Annual Report and Mrs Edmonds remembers Miss Mitchell teaching her how to read and correct proofs.

The Committee itself was very informal. It was made up of 16 members. If one had to retire someone else known to be interested in town planning was invited to join. There seem to have been no elections. Miss Mitchell came in to Glasgow fairly often. At first she came in her own car, but later she came by bus 'to let the professionals do the driving', as she put it. Before a meeting of the Committee Miss Mitchell and the Assistant Secretary went over the business, especially if any letters had to be sent to the press. The other work was shared among the members. Miss Mitchell herself was very quiet and retiring and there were few, if any, stories about her though she could fight like a lion over a matter if principle. She was, however, so quiet and courteous that there was never any bad blood.

Sir William Whyte of Lanarkshire was unanimously elected President and the seven Vice Presidents included Miss E.B. Mitchell, J.P., while the Hon. Secretary was Bailie Mrs Jean Mann. The Committee also included the distinguished journalist William Power. Mrs Mann and Miss Mitchell drew together on the executive committee of the infant Scottish branch, though Miss Mitchell may have been a little shocked when, after Mrs Mann declared in the City Chambers that she wanted a new town, a local paper reported 'Mann wants but little here below'. But it was Miss Mitchell who quoted this with approval in an article in *Town and Country Planning*.[2] In 1938 Mrs Mann and Miss Mitchell organised an unofficial tour for twenty Glasgow councillors to see Letchworth and Welwyn. Mrs Mann organised the tour and Miss Mitchell covered the cost of the transport. The visit was a great success and the councillors said they had been much impressed by what they had seen. In the same year the main Garden City and Town Planning Association held its annual conference in Glasgow as part of the Empire Exhibition and arranged for the delegates to visit Aberdeen, Dundee, Dunfermline and Edinburgh to see what was being done to rehouse slum dwellers. Osborne spoke and said that the people believed the local authorities had the right aims, but were not working properly to achieve them. He believed that the local authorities themselves had completely wrong aims which they were working with most damnable efficiency to achieve. The speech made an enormous impression on the young Robert (later Professor Sir Robert) Grieve.

The autumn of 1938 saw the Munich crisis and the fear of a World War but this war was averted for the moment. The outstanding event during the summer for the planners had been the creation of a Royal Commission to consider the redistribution of industry. Among many other organisations that gave evidence to this committee including the Royal Burghs of Scotland, and the Letchworth and Welwyn Companies, was the Garden City and Town Planning Association. Their evidence was described by the General Secretary of P.E.P.[3] as 'an able and devastating document'.

The following autumn the Association made the first presentation of the Howard Medal to Sir Raymond Unwin who had worked very closely with Howard. The Association held a conference in Cardiff where the unanimous demand for planning showed a great change in public opinion. But the year was 1939 and by September Britain was at war with Germany. For some time planners had been worried at the damage which could be done to a city by bombs. Photographs from Spain appeared in *Town and Country Planning*, the film of H.G. Wells' book about war in the air was in the cinemas, and people had been officially issued with gasmasks. On 'Frightful Friday' children evacuated from Glasgow's Townhead arrived in Biggar and children from Bridgeton came to Symington.

In 1940, in spite of the war, a report was produced by the Royal Commission on the Geographical Distribution of Industrial Population, the

Barlow Report. On the whole it supported the ideas that had been put forward by the Garden City and Town Planning Association. A meeting in Glasgow in March was addressed by Sir William Whyte, Professor J.H. Jones, Sir John Stirling Maxwell and F.J. Osborn and was well covered in the Scottish press. The Report provided an opportunity to consider such basic problems of housing policy as garden cities, satellite cities and trading estates. The Scottish branch of the Garden City and Town Planning Association was very active. By this time the branch had made contact with John Wardhaugh of the Glasgow Treelovers Association of which society Miss Mitchell was a founder member. She was now Chairman of the Executive Committee of the Scottish branch of the GCTPA. She saw the Association as 'distinctively propagandist' and remembered what Sir Theodore Chambers had said to her on one of her visits to Welwyn: that the planners must aim at convincing the politicians and the public. This she set about doing. There were monthly discussion meetings in Glasgow, as there were in London. and the Scottish Branch held its own annual conferences. The one at Largs in 1941 Miss Mitchell thought was the first one to be successful. 1941 was a year when *Town and Country Planning* noted that never in history had there been so much talk of planning. Sir William Whyte, who had been very active in housing during the 1914–18 war, was now heading the movement for planning. The architect Robert Hurd supported the need for planning and amenities and warned that houses for the working class must not take the shape of regularly dreary colonies like Niddrie near Edinburgh.

The main branch of the Town and Country Planning Association decided to produce a series of books published by the important firm Faber & Faber. Lady Rhondda, the proprietor of the weekly *Time and Tide*, warmly commended them. The BBC ran a series on 'Making Plans' and Julian Huxley, on the Brains Trust, supported the idea of Garden Cities and recommended the periodical *Town and Country Planning*. The Church supported the idea of planning, the Bishop of Winchester pointing out the need for garden city communities with churches, libraries, clubs and space, while the Bishop of London pointed out the danger of segregating people according to wealth. The Archbishop of York urged the creation of new cities and the dispersal of industries. The Industrial Christian Fellowship urged a united planning authority.

The Saltire Society of which Robert Hurd was the moving spirit was also active in Scotland in stirring up interest in town and country planning and issued a pamphlet by the Principal of Dundee School of Economics. They also created an award for the best new houses built by a local authority.

But though there was much support for national planning and Reports appeared on Compensation for land needed for housing (Uthwait) and on the need to protect agricultural land (Scott) there was an absence of decision by the government. The promise of a new Town Planning Ministry was overshadowed by the Beveridge Report. But in Scotland in 1943 Miss Mitchell felt that things were beginning to move fast. Tom Johnston, Secretary of State for Scotland in Churchill's Coalition Government, managed to persuade the authorities of Glasgow, the surrounding counties and the larger burghs, to sink their differences and rivalries and join together as the Clyde Valley Regional Planning Advisory Committee. The final report was never definitely adopted by the Committee but what became known as the Abercrombie/Matthew Report contained very important recommendations for a green belt round Glasgow and four new towns to relieve overcrowding. The towns proposed were at East Kilbride, Cumbernauld, Bishopton and Houston.

The election of 1945 turned out the Coalition Government and put in a Labour Government under Attlee. The Town and Country Planning Association pointed out that planners must impress on the new government that legislation to make dispersal planning a reality could not possibly wait. The Government had still to declare its policy based on the Reports of Barlow, Uthwatt and Scott. In 1945 a New Town Committee was set up under Lord Reith but planners felt that long before this, sites should have been taken and work started.

In 1946 the New Town Committee reported and this was followed by the New Town Act which, as Miss Mitchell emphasised, was a non-party measure. The new Secretary of State for Scotland, 'wee Joe Westwood', was a firm supporter of policy advocated by the Town and Country Planning Association.

When a new town at East Kilbride was first proposed Glasgow Corporation opposed the whole project. The City Engineer, Robert Bruce, produced a different plan. It claimed that it could rehouse its whole, at present congested, population within its own boundaries. It said that only 98,000 houses were needed and that of these only 50,000 need be new and that when these houses had been built the housing problem of the city would have been solved. The 1946 Department of Health estimate that 100,000 houses were needed was scaled down by Glasgow because when some overcrowded families moved out, their accommodation could be used by smaller families. The figure of 98,000 was based on the number of names on the waiting list and Glasgow thought that some of these applications for new houses were not very serious, saying that some people wanted to move because they could not get their taps repaired. St Andrew's House was not impressed. They pointed out that in 1935 there had been 148,000 houses out of 280,000 which consisted of only two, or even one, room and that once families had been removed, these 'houses' should never be used again. Mr Westwood did not think the application for 98,000 houses was frivolous. The Census of 1951 showed the congestion in Glasgow was worse than anywhere else in Britain. This confirmed the Clyde Valley Plan figures of 1946.

Another of Glasgow's objections to the proposed new town was that it would affect twenty-five farmers producing half a million gallons of milk per annum and that taking into consideration the Corporation's own plan to build on agricultural land at Castlemilk and Garscadden this would involve a loss that could not be borne. Again Mr Westwood was not impressed. He decided that East Kilbride should be developed south of the main road and railway and that development at Castlemilk should be limited to 1,000 acres. He estimated that the amount of milk available would in fact be 750,000 gallons per annum.

The Secretary of State decided that there was a *prima facie* case for a new town in Lanarkshire. The Town and Country Planning Association (Scottish Section) rejoiced and declared that 'the battle for a new town in the Clyde Valley had been won'.[4]

Glasgow City Council's opposition was defeated largely because of the skill and determination of James McGuinness of the Department of Health. In May 1947 a designation order was made setting up a Development Corporation of eight people to create the new town of East Kilbride. Mrs Mann and Gilbert McAllister had now both become M.P.s so they would have less time to devote to the problems of overcrowding in Glasgow but on their recommendations Miss Mitchell was nominated as 'the woman' on the Corporation. At first she had some misgivings as to her suitability; as she said herself, she had never been a 'housewife' and she was sixty-five years old, but her enthusiasm for the new town outweighed all her misgivings. In August the members of the Corporation met the Secretary of State for Scotland and he instructed them as to their powers and gave them the signal to go.

They went that afternoon to look at the site. East Kilbride lay about ten miles south of Glasgow with the road to Paisley on the west and the road to Coatbridge and Airdrie east across the river Calder. It stood in hills sloping north and its situation was very like that of Cathkin which William Power had suggested as the ideal new town. Mains Castle to the north had been given to John Lindsay for his help in murdering the Red Comyn. Torrance House had been the home of the Stuarts of Castlemilk.

The Corporation were fortunate in their Chairman, Sir Patrick Dollan. During the war he had been Lord Provost of Glasgow but he was so genuinely interested in the need to relieve Glasgow's overcrowding that in 1941, even in the middle of the war, he had found time to write an article for *Town and Country Planning* on the best way of solving overcrowding in Scotland's Middle Belt. He wanted Clydebank to be as beautiful as any garden city and had urged that if this was to be achieved pre-war parochialism must be abandoned and Clydeside seen as one economic and industrial community from Larkhill in the East to Inverkip in the West and that existing services must be exploited so that new towns did not have to be built up from nothing.

That the new East Kilbride Development Corporation was able to make use of existing transport and other facilities was due partly to the work already done by the Clyde Valley Regional Planning Advisory Committee and partly to the fact that Sir John Mann, Chairman of the Lanarkshire County Council, was the Vice Chairman of the new East Kilbride Development Corporation. He had come to Lanarkshire as a railwayman and had been elected to the county council as a young man, to become its first Labour Chairman, respected by all the members on the council and by St. Andrews House.

The other members of the Corporation were the architect S. Bunton; the Chartered Accountant A.G. McBain; the Chairman of the Scottish Special Housing Association, W.A. McPhail; the Director of the Scottish Cooperative Wholesale Society, J.B. Mavor; the Chairman of Mavor & Coulson, the engineering firm which had already moved from Glasgow to East Kilbride; and H.T. McCalman, a Glasgow solicitor who had been on the Glasgow Corporation since 1935, had been Convenor of the Highways & Planning Committee 1943–48, and Chairman of the Clyde Valley Regional Planning Advisory Committee.

Miss Mitchell felt that the fact that East Kilbride was to go ahead in spite of the country's post-war financial difficulties was of first class importance to the planning movement because 'the battle for East Kilbride is the main battle for the principles of the Green Belt and the relief of congestion in the big cities by grouping development beyond the Green Belt.'[5]

One September afternoon in 1947 the Corporation paid a second visit to the village. They visited the works of Mavor and Coulson which before the war had been moved from Bridgeton. At this second meeting, the Chairman, Sir Patrick Dollan, produced the news that two large properties, Torrance House with its policies in the West and Thorntonhall and its policies in the east of East Kilbride, were available for purchase. Some of the Corporation were staggered by this and thought it was too early to acquire such premises but these objections were overruled and the houses with the land round them were bought. Miss Mitchell commented that 'if we were really going to build a new town the opportunity of securing such accommodation ready made was as precious as diamonds'.[6]

Staff were recruited: Major General B.E.C. Dixon to be general manager, J.H. McLusky as secretary and legal advisor, D.G. Malcolm as chief estates officer, D.P. Gray to be chief architect and planning officer and J. Brown the chief finance officer. In May 1948 Lady Dollan opened Torrance House as the offices of the Corporation. In the same year Miss Mitchell could report that the dreams of yesterday were becoming the visible fabric of everyday life as on 12 June, sandwiched between the East Kilbride Agricultural Show and the young Farmers' Gymkhana, the new town made its first appearance in the shape of a model exhibition opened by the Secretary of State for Scotland. The same day Miss Mitchell marked the site of the first new building by knocking in a peg at Whitemoss where new buildings

Miss Mitchell knocking in the first peg at East Kilbride, 1948
by kind permission of East Kilbride Development Corporation

would join the existing village. The press photograph shows her looking very like Grandma in the Giles cartoons with the Secretary of State for Scotland, by this time Arthur Woodburn, holding the peg and Sir Patrick Dollan looking on. Miss Mitchell felt that Fortune had smiled almost dangerously on the first Scottish new town. The cooperation of the departments of state and Lanarkshire County Council had been most encouraging and the decision of the Department of Scientific and Industrial Research (UK) to establish their Mechanical Engineering Research Laboratory (MERL) in Thorntonhall had been most encouraging.

Up to 1949 there had already been 7,000 applications for houses. 68 nontraditional houses had been built close to the existing village and in 1949 124 more nontraditional houses. These would be houses with casement rather than sash windows and a pebble and dash finish on the walls. They would not be of stone and the roofs might be of some synthetic material rather than slate or thatch. Traditional houses would be begun probably in 1950 in which year possibly 450 houses would be put up. The Corporation was in favour of terraced houses, partly because these were usual in Scotland and partly because they were well adapted to the climate.

One difficulty confronting the New Town was that rent for a four-room house would be £40 per month whereas rent for a similar house put up by the Lanarkshire County Council was only £23.

From the very first, Miss Mitchell encouraged an interest in trees and in hedgerows which she urged should be kept and used instead of fences. In the field at Whitemoss, where she had driven in the peg to mark the corner of the first house, there were very few trees but the street was planned to keep what there were. The various architects, Lockhart Hutson, Alan Reiach and J. Coia all took care to preserve what trees there were. When a landscape consultant came to advise, she planned shelter belts especially in the south-west and used hardy trees that would do well in that particular soil and with that exposure. Soon a tree nursery was started at Torrance House. A visiting deputation which came to inspect the sites one bitter March could hardly endure the wind, especially as at that stage the sites had to be visited on foot across fields for the roads had not yet been built.

In the areas intended for housing the most level parts were noted as suitable for schools.

One feature of the plan was to have great roundabouts on the main roads. Sir Patrick Dollan was inclined to question these roundabouts and also the pedestrian underpasses as too big and too expensive but a police officer from Glasgow assured him that in time he would be very thankful to have them.

Miss Mary Mackenzie was appointed house management assistant and did a great deal to preserve the character of the old village and to help newcomers to settle in happily. One of the features of the town in the early days which helped to develop a feeling of community was the Willow Tea Room of Mr and Mrs Mackay in a little group of buildings designed by Alan Reiach and with a large mature tree beside it.

One of the problems was how to allocate houses. First on the list were men working at Mavor and Coulson who were still living in Bridgeton. The Corporation was very reluctant for the new town to become a dormitory for people working in Glasgow and they did what they could to prevent this though eventually about half the population worked outside the town. One problem that the Corporation had not considered was whether to admit older people, even those who had retired. Later it was felt that if they were not included the population might be rather young and all of one age group.

Great satisfaction was felt when Rolls Royce began to build works in Nerston industrial estate to the north of the old village near the works of Mavor and Coulson. Miss Mitchell was delighted when she was shown round the MERL[7] works of the Department of Scientific and Industrial Research to find windows that let in sunshine, plenty of ventilation and attractively coloured walls. Now that steam and coal were no longer necessary to provide power it was much easier to have clean and bright factories.

In January 1950 *Town and Country Planning* carried a most helpful article by Miss Elizabeth about the New Town together with a clear map. The plan of the new town was a triangle bounded by the main roads to Glasgow on the north, to Hamilton on the east and to Strathavon on the south. There would be four wards: the old village; Westwood in the west; Calderwood in the east; and Murray in the south. Each ward would have its own schools and shops. There would be two industrial estates, one to the west where the Department of Scientific and Industrial Research had already decided to site its Mechanical Engineering Research Laboratory, making use at the outset of some war-time temporary buildings at Thorntonhall. The other industrial estate would be in the north at Nerston where 60 acres would be available for private factories. The Corporation offices were in Torrance House. The main problem at that stage was housing. Already the enormous number of 7,000 applications had been received and so far only 124 non-traditional houses had been built though in the course of 1950 it was hoped to build 400 houses in Murray Ward. It was hoped that by 1952 there would be accommodation for people employed in other industries and Miss

Elizabeth pointed out that it was essential that a beginning to provide these industries should be made at once. Two problems confronting the New Town were the location of the road to the south of the centre and the fact that rents were higher in the New Town than on houses built by Lanarkshire County Council. There was also the difficulty that Glasgow and Rutherglen were building outside their rateable area. The Development Corporation was pressing the Secretary of State to consider this. It was encouraging for the Development Corporation that the report of their first year had been approved by such distinguished experts as Sir Patrick Abercrombie, Sir Frank Mann and Professor Holford.

Progress continued though such fundamental things as main drains provided little to see. The main feature that could be observed was the great building going up for the D.S.I.R. The houses completed as part of the first programme were giving satisfaction, especially the system of group heating. A few mature trees gave a settled look to the houses, more especially since the first gardens and green verges had been made. In March there had been a very happy tree-planting ceremony when East Kilbride children marched out in large numbers each to plant a little tree 'with the intention of boasting to their grandchildren.'[9] The Glasgow Treelovers Society had provided some young trees. Miss Elizabeth recorded with satisfaction that a community association was being formed.

In the autumn of 1950 the bulldozers wallowed in mire worthy of comparison with the legends of Letchworth and Welwyn. In June 1950 an important advance had been made when permission had been given to go ahead with site preparation for the Board of Trade industrial estate. Work on the first private factory, a small one, would begin soon. On the industrial site in the south the roofing stage of the big general purposes building for MERL had been reached and other MERL buildings had their steel structure complete. Miss Elizabeth noted that 'both north and south of the centre (still undeveloped) it is now plain that the new town will be a town and not a suburb'.[10]

By October 1950 196 houses had been built, 167 were under construction and 137 had been contracted for but not begun. So far all the houses built had had four rooms but in 1951 it was expected to build in a variety of styles even including some three-storey blocks of flats and there would be smaller houses in the old village. Allocation of houses still presented problems. Men essential for work in DSIR obviously had a good claim to be considered, as had employees of the Development Corporation, and people ill-housed or over-crowded in the old village and workers already employed in East Kilbride but living in Glasgow.

So far the shops, school and churches in the village had sufficed to serve the new town but from 1951 several groups of shops were planned for the Murray area near the MERL works and another group was to be built in the centre. There was talk of an office for the S.W. Scotland Electricity Board, a hotel, even possibly a cinema, but nothing had yet been decided. A site had been allocated to the Church of Scotland, and negotiations were in progress with the Roman Catholics and Episcopalians. Plans to create amenities were progressing. A scrap of land had been made into a playground for toddlers and another had been made into a rest garden for the elderly. By the end of 1950 development was about to begin in the centre. An earlier difficulty about the east-west road had been resolved, but the differences in the level of rents in the New Town and houses built by Lanarkshire County Council continued and a new problem had become more serious for the Board of Trade was reluctant to provide new industries to a town where there was no unemployment. Miss Elizabeth remarked sharply:

> This is to ignore the Barlow Report, the New Town Act and the whole policy of planned dispersal. New towns are a special case requiring rapid development in the housing and industrial side simultaneously, and it takes two years to build a factory.[11]

In 1951 there was a change of Government and there was a serious danger that the new town might be scrapped, but development had gone too far for that to be possible.

Visitors admired the roundabouts and underpasses. The members of the Corporation had, perhaps, not realised what a high proportion of pedestrians were mothers with prams or toddlers. Other visitors remarked that the houses were not for workers but for the middle class. There were indeed some 'managerial' houses with six rooms and a garage but all the houses were designed for people of the same species. The town had nooks and surprises known only to the residents. It achieved a good balance between traditional living conditions and twentieth-century traffic. The groups of houses near Brousterland, the oldest house in the village, were particularly attractive. Markethill had a felicitous mixture of flats and family houses and old people's cottages. The fine wooded ravine of the Calder was particularly attractive and so was the little new Headhouse Parkway in one of the shallow valleys up on the plateau.

At the beginning of 1952 Miss Elizabeth was able to make an encouraging report. One thing which had helped East Kilbride was the continuity of the members of the Corporation. After four years, six of the original eight were still in office and Sir Patrick Dollan and Sir John Mann were still Chairman and Vice-chairman respectively.

The chief officials were also still in place. Industrial development was well ahead. MERL was working in its new building and other buildings were going up which would occupy the whole of the site at the south-east of the town. When these were complete there would be jobs for 700 men. At Nerston in the north-east site preparations were nearly complete for a Rolls Royce jet engine factory which it was expected would employ 3,500, of whom 75% would be men. Most of the rest of Nerston was booked by John Deere of Illinois, agricultural engineers who expected to have jobs for 2,000 people, mostly men. The European manager of this firm was already living in the town. 'So large and sudden an expansion of industry employment will for a time be ahead of housing',[12] but Miss Elizabeth was confident that housing would soon draw level.

The road system was taking shape. An east-west road would link the radial roads from the old village and was expected to be in use shortly. The main north-south roads would eventually by-pass the village and restore some of its ancient peace. By October 1951, 296 houses had been completed and occupied of which twelve were managerial. 158 were under construction and in 1952 it was expected to start 1,000 houses and flats. Some people wanted high flats built in the Murray district but Miss Elizabeth was very doubtful about their suitability. Would they cast long shadows on other houses? Would all the tenants have orderly habits and would there be no young children? She concluded that if all these conditions were met 'there may be no compelling objection to a few tall blocks, but their erection, if decided, will be an experiment and not a policy'.[13]

She reported that the Scottish Committee of the Council of Industrial Design had staged a charming exhibition of decorations and furniture but with her usual commonsense and her unerring knack of putting her fingers on a weak spot she added:

> ought there, perhaps, to be another exhibition house fitted up with special thought for a father in heavy industry and hearty boys of 10-12 – more in the tradition of the old Scottish cottage with the sturdy, homelike beauty?[14]

She noted with regret that sodium street lighting, while it gave even distribution of light, was very ugly. But on the positive side she recorded that, in spite of rents in the New Town being higher than in some council houses, the Corporation had no difficulty in finding tenants. She also recorded with satisfaction that, though there was not money yet to provide outside amenities, much-needed tennis courts had been provided thanks to the District Council.

In 1953 she was able to write with satisfaction that

> from being a project, new East Kilbride has become a plan. People can come and sit in the little tree-shaded restaurant, beside the shops and the wide pavement and look along a smooth road to the quiet roundabout which will be the hub of the town . . . They can move round the town instead of exploring out radially from the old village into disconnected scenes of chaos, full of mud and bulldozers. So also, nobody need ask now 'What about employment in the new town?' Where a year ago, on the Nerston industrial estate, there was a great sea of mud, there are now the great Rolls Royce workshops, partly already at work. Then the public can now begin to see what is meant by a planned new town.[15]

She had been astonished at the industries of new East Kilbride 'which have sprung up like something in the Arabian Nights'.[16] What delighted her particularly were 'The harmonious, pleasing colours of the workshops. The blue grey machine tools, the light quiet walls, the deep red doors'.[17]

In July 1953 Miss Elizabeth's six years as a member of the Development Corporation came to an end and it nearly broke her heart. 'It reminded me of being torn from the big brick box in the Doune Terrace nursery,[18] but she reminded herself that 'all those delightful years had been beyond the proper retiring age.'[19]

By 1953, when Miss Mitchell's third term of office came to an end, two of the industrial sites were filling up and two of the residential quarters, Murray in the south and West Mains in the north, were developing fast with houses, schools and churches. Sir Patrick Dollan was implacably opposed to multi-storey building and young families from Glasgow preferred houses at ground floor level. The Corporation had no flats of more than four storeys and did their best to keep to this height of flats as far as the higher powers would allow. The houses were built more compactly than had been the practice in the first two new towns in England. In East Kilbride there were more terraces and fewer detached houses, with some continuous low housing of one, two or three storeys. This had been the Scottish tradition except in Edinburgh and some of the other large towns and had the advantage of moderating the wind and letting in the sun.

Miss Mitchell remained vividly interested in her New Town and in 1957 when East Kilbride celebrated its tenth anniversary she could report the occasion with great satisfaction. The Minister of State, Lord Strathclyde, outlined a policy for the future which might have come out of the pages of *Town and Country Planning*. The success of East Kilbride and Glenrothes was more important for Scotland than the success of the new towns in England because England already had the examples of Letchworth and Welwyn whereas in Scotland East Kilbride was something completely new.

If Miss Elizabeth was sorry to stop work at East Kilbride, East Kilbride was as sorry to see her go. The members and the officials of the Development Corporation expressed their gratitude and affection by presenting her with a plaque of the arms of the New Town. At the top of the shield was a chequered band, one half being blue and white for the Stuarts of Torrance and the other black and white for the Maxwells of Calderwood. The main part of the shield was divided in half with a cogwheel on a black background on one side representing industry and on the other, a blazing sun on a green ground representing agriculture. At the bottom of the shield was a cross for St. Bride. In 1975 a new coat of arms was designed by the Lord Lyon. This omitted the cogwheel and the blazing sun but added two white stars for Lindsay of Mains Castle, who had been Lords of the Manor till the seventeenth century. At the base of the new shield was an oyster-catcher, a bird associated with St. Bride, and it was shown with a background half of gold for the wealth created by industry and half of green for the agricultural village. Sir Patrick Dollan, when he presented Miss Mitchell with the plaque, spoke of her fifty years of service as a pioneer in housing, education, local government, politics and afforestation. It was largely thanks to her that 150,000 trees had been planted in and around East Kilbride. An inscription on the plaque mentioned the 'splendid service she has given as a member of the Corporation'.[20] Characteristically Miss Mitchell planted a tree outside Torrance House.

In December 1955 the Town & Country Planning Association conferred on Miss Elizabeth what she described as 'an undreamed of honour'[21] by presenting her with the Ebenezer Howard Medal. This was awarded only occasionally to someone who had made a particularly outstanding contribution to the work of the association. The presentation was made by Sir Patrick Abercrombie, himself a winner of the medal, at a dinner in the House of Commons. Miss Elizabeth's health was proposed by the Scottish Minister of State, who later became Lord Craigton, and seconded by Sir Frederick Osborn whose speech at the Town and Country Planning meeting in Glasgow had so impressed the young Robert Grieve and who had had a

Howard Medal
by kind permission of Biggar Museum

long career in town planning including involvement in Letchworth, being
the first estate manager of Welwyn, Chairman of the Executive of the Town
and Country Planning Association of Great Britain, and Editor for many
years of the *Town and Country Planning* magazine. The Minister of State
spoke of her devoted work for the Scottish Section of the Town and
Country Planning Association and said that it well deserved to be called
'distinguished'. He went on to say that she had been able to achieve so much
because of her 'charming and sincere personality as well as her informed
and tactful advocacy'. Perhaps it was an indication of Miss Elizabeth's
sincere modesty that whereas when other people had been given the Howard
Medal their pictures had appeared in *Town and Country Planning* and there
had been considerable publicity, no picture appeared of Miss Elizabeth and
there was only half a column in a report on various other town planning
matters.

Miss Mitchell, 1955
by kind permission of Biggar Museum press cuttings

But just because Miss Elizabeth was no longer a member of the East Kilbride Development Corporation it did not mean that she was less active in promoting town planning. In 1952 the Town Development Act had been passed but it applied only to England and Wales. The Scots expected a Scottish Bill to follow and when nothing happened Mrs Jean Mann, M.P. for Coatbridge asked a question in the House. In November 1952, the Secretary of State replied that there was no particular overspill problem in Scotland. As late as 1952 Glasgow Corporation had still assumed that its congested population could be rehoused within the city boundaries and the Bruce Plan made this point. It was prepared to sacrifice the green belt and build high rise flats but it did not appreciate that the total area of Glasgow was too small for a population of over 1,000,000 which meant that the area per head was the smallest in Great Britain. The Abercrombie Report in 1946 had advocated four new towns to relieve the overcrowded working class homes of Glasgow. In 1952, Mr Jury, the city architect and town planner, produced a report saying that 129,000 new houses were needed. He was the first official of this status in Glasgow and his appointment had been actively pressed by the Scottish Office. Miss Elizabeth in *Town and Country*

Planning urged that Mr Jury's new towns must not be dormitory settlements based on exhausting daily journeys to and from work. East Kilbride had shown that a new town could be a place of living and working and it was essential that the second crop of new towns should be rooted in the same principles.

In 1952 Glasgow Corporation produced a plan which had been prepared a number of months earlier proposing more building on the outskirts over what remained of the green belt and making no mention of the need to take a quarter of a million people out of Glasgow if conditions for the remaining citizens were to be made decent. The County of Lanark and the Town and Country Planning Association (Scottish Section) opposed this plan.

The public enquiry into the proposal was remarkable. Hugh T. McCalman B.L., a member of the East Kilbride Development Corporation and former member of the Clyde Valley Regional Planning Advisory Committee, acted for the Town and Country Planning Association (Scottish Section), as Miss Elizabeth put it, 'for love of the cause'. One of the witnesses was 'the great Sir Patrick Abercrombie himself'.[22] Miss Elizabeth was the other witness for the Town and Country Planning Association (Scottish Section). She was, after all, the chairman of the executive committee.

> It was an extraordinary occasion, with the flower of the Scottish Bar engaged on one side or the other, and the citizens of Glasgow showing no interest whatever.[23]

Miss Elizabeth admitted that for her

> it was a new experience to be cross-examined by a Q.C. but our case was so good and we were long familiar with it that we could not well go wrong.[24]

She might have added that for over a quarter of a century she had been herself a J.P. and that as the daughter of a Sheriff Substitute she was not likely to be intimidated by even the most distinguished lawyers.

The industrialists in the old areas in Glasgow feared that developments of their factories would be hindered if areas were zoned for housing. There were some objections to planning of any sort. Lanarkshire objected to building which might obliterate the green belt between Glasgow and the industrial centres.

A little movement seemed apparent in 1953. The Secretary of State asked the reconstituted Clyde Valley Advisory Council to report on the problem of overspill. Miss Elizabeth noted that this was good as far as it went but the question was not only regional but national. She regretted that 'all this stir had not been six years ago, but better late than never'.[25] The Glasgow Corporation had not yet accepted the Jury Report but there were signs that it was moving in this direction.

1953, 1954 and 1955 saw pressure building up for a new town. The *Glasgow Herald* was 'a wonderful ally producing a stream of articles and leaders and TCPA letters'.[26] Miss Mitchell had close contacts with the press.

The reappointed Clyde Valley Planning Advisory Committee, the Housing and Town Planning Council, and the Scottish Council for Development and Industry all urged the need for a new town. Then, in the summer of 1954 Robert Grieve (later Professor Sir Robert) spoke at a Town Planning Institute Conference at St. Andrews on the Abercrombie Report. This address seems to have convinced some of the politicians in St. Andrew's House. But there were further delays. Glasgow Corporation wanted a new town under the New Town Act financed by the Government, but the Secretary of State wanted Glasgow to contribute for every house occupied by someone on the Glasgow housing list and to feu one third of the overall deficits on the scheme. In return Glasgow would elect one third of the members of the Development Corporation and Dumbarton would elect another third.

The Scottish Section of the Town and Country Planning Association expressed some sympathy with Glasgow. The rates there were very high and the rateable value per head was low. Miss Elizabeth in *Town and Country Planning* pointed out that at East Kilbride

> the development corporation was and is made up of individuals widely varying but chosen and appointed to preserve single mindedly the best possible development of the new town, not to represent this or that outside interest. Divisions of opinion, when they occurred did not run on political or municipal lines . . . It would seem to be poor economy to delay an urgently necessary enterprise and depart from a tried method in hopes of wringing a money contribution from an unwilling Glasgow which honestly, in view of future needs, cannot afford it.[27]

The Town and Country Planning Association (Scottish Section) wrote to the Secretary of State stressing the ever-increasing urgency for a new town, the desirability and justice of using the New Town Act and national finance, and the urgent need for preparatory measures for wider dispersal of some of the Glasgow overspill. Still nothing happened. Both sides seemed too proud to move a step.

At this point the Town and Country Planning Association (Scottish Section) burst in with the widest possible publicity appealing to the Secretary of State to use the New Town Act on this occasion seeing that the relief already secured for Glasgow was so grossly disproportionate to what had been given to London. The Association urged Glasgow's Corporation to pocket their pride and sense of injustice and contribute something for houses that would be occupied by Glasgow people.[28]

The Association was quoted in the House of Commons and in July 1955 a draft designation order for Cumbernauld was issued under the New Town Act. This New Town had to accept a higher density of building because it was bounded by local mines between its hilly site and Glasgow, and on the other side by clay mines. In the autumn the Town and Country Planning Association (Scottish Section) again wrote to the Secretary of State. While it welcomed the recent order designating Cumbernauld a new town it respectfully urged that the movement of industry was the crucial planning question at the present time and that in regard to the nominations of tenants by Glasgow Corporation the Association regarded it of high importance that the new town should not be directly linked with the slum clearance in Glasgow but should be free to draw a mixed population willing and qualified to work in the new town, i.e. applicants not necessarily high in the Glasgow housing list.[29] The Association went on to point out, as it had done before, that emigration of individuals and families

> is hampered and almost prevented by the fact that the provision of new housing is almost entirely in the hands of local authorities.[30]

This letter, signed by Miss Elizabeth as Chairman of the Executive of the Town and Country Planning Association (Scottish Section) and by H.J. Crone as Hon. Secretary, was not only published in full in *Town and Country Planning* but had an ominous note at the bottom to the effect that it was proposed to send a copy of this letter to the press.

In March 1956 the Development Corporation for Cumbernauld New Town was set up with Lt. Gen. Sir Gordon Macmillan as chairman. As Miss Elizabeth recorded, the battle was over. Through *Town and Country Planning* she sent good wishes to the new Corporation especially that it might be united and keen in spirit. She urged the importance of developing industries and building schools as well as houses, and hoped that there would be a mixed varied population able to work and have their main social interest in the new town. She warned the Corporation yet again to keep clear of the idea of an outer suburb or housing schemes and to encourage the various 'homeless' young couples of various types and callings, insisting that it was essential to have a mixed population, not a group sent out *en masse* from a particular part of Glasgow.

At first the Cumbernauld Corporation had offices in Glasgow but before the end of 1956 they had acquired Cumbernauld House and the estate from 'a willing but reluctant' seller, Colonel Alan Burns. As in the case of East Kilbride this large immediate acquisition greatly helped the work of the Corporation. One of the first problems at Cumbernauld was the pressure to build high rise flats. Miss Elizabeth pointed out that in East Kilbride people preferred houses which could be entered at ground level. She warned:

> It will be a disaster if the cramped families of Glasgow, seeking to escape to freedom, are piled up again as if they were bees or ants.[31]

The houses in Seafar, on the west side of the New Town, showed what could be done to avoid tower blocks and crowded houses. She noted that the Corporation was putting up a good fight and wondered whether the Scottish Town Development Bill would come powerfully to their aid 'and how soon?'

In 1957 when Cumbernauld was only a year old Miss Elizabeth noted that the first large factory was being built and recorded with regret that one of the new town's main difficulties was the exact line of the roads A8 and A73. The A73 was at present a planner's nightmare, for it cut through the middle of the town. This year saw the Housing and Town Development (Scotland) Act and the Minister of State authorised a policy of dispersal that might have come from the pages of *Town and Country Planning* itself. Miss Elizabeth noted, possibly with a twinkle in her eye, 'strange to think back to 1952, when the powers imagined that no overspill problem existed in Scotland.'[32] Cumbernauld was still confronted by the problem of what line was to be taken by the A73 and the demand that, because of the rather difficult site, houses should be built closer together than in many new towns and that there should be more high rise flats. Miss Elizabeth again warned against high rise flats and cited the experience of East Kilbride which indicated

> a very strong general desire for cottage or terrace houses; the simple likeable houses that have helped to draw a cheerful, youthful population.[33]

She concluded with the warning: 'Time will show the social effects of high rise flats and the proportion desirable.' She added that after the first development it would always be possible to modify plans if necessary. The second problem in the New Town was relations with Glasgow and Miss Elizabeth realised that what the Victorians called 'sanctified common sense' would be badly needed when the time came to allocate houses.

In October 1957 Miss Elizabeth had wondered whether the work of the Town and Country Planning Association (Scottish Section) was ended. When the Secretary of State cut the first sod at Cumbernauld he had said he was not opposed to the idea of another new town. By this time Glasgow Corporation was aware of the need to move people out into existing towns, even such remote ones as Haddington and Kirkentilloch or Grangemouth.[34] But she concluded that there was still a long road ahead with some awkward corners. For most of 1958 she contributed to reports on developments in Scotland while she waited and watched how Development Corporations and Local Authorities acted under the Town Development (Scotland) Act of 1957. East Kilbride and Glenrothes had almost ceased to be news but Cumbernauld had not yet found its distinctive character. It was planned for close development, urbanism and high rise flats though as yet the flats had not been built. Miss Elizabeth pointed out that the Corporation

> has not yet encountered the mass resistance which has kept the two
> earlier new towns down to earth. The first towers in a Scottish new town
> will be an experiment to watch.[35]

She noted with wry amusement that the people in favour of multi-storey flats and communal services were usually Conservatives while members of the Labour Party tended to support the idea of a man's 'own private castle with front and back door on the ground and a private scrap of earth.'[36]

Miss Elizabeth remained deeply worried about the overcrowded conditions in Glasgow. Legislation had been passed. Opinion had changed drastically at St. Andrew's House and in the Glasgow City Chambers where Councillors were clamouring for new towns and actively supporting dispersal of people and of industries but there were still protests reminiscent of the days before the Jury Report of 1952.

> As in the case of the high flats of Cumbernauld, so with dispersal from
> Gorbals, Bridgeton and Glasgow generally, the first steps of the
> movement will provide useful experience.[37]

In 1959 Miss Elizabeth retired as Chairman of the Executive of the T.C.P.A. (Scottish Section). She could look back on many changes since she had first become a member, many of them affecting the Highlands. There was the policy of reafforestation which had been initiated by Lord Lovat. There had been the hydroelectric schemes initiated by Tom Johnson when he was Secretary of State. Then there had appeared the Highlands and Islands Development Board. The Chairman of the Board, Sir Robert Grieve, knew Miss Mitchell well and admired her enormously. His first two years as Chairman of the Highlands and Islands Development Board were very difficult and when he was at a very low ebb he was delighted and his confidence was restored when Miss Mitchell wrote him a letter of warm appreciation and sent him a packet of Sanatogen. He took the Sanatogen but it was the letter that restored his morale.[38] In the south there had been the long battle to relieve overcrowding in Glasgow and the creation of new towns, the latest of which, Livingston, began in 1962. But in that year Miss Elizabeth was ill and had to retire.

[1] This is also based on Reports written by Miss Mitchell for *Town and Country Planning* magazine. Some are signed, some are not, but all read very much as if written by her.
[2] *Town and Country Planning* 1940 vol. 18.
[3] Political & Economic Planning, a 'think tank' very active in the '30s. 'Devastating' for those opposed to the redistribution of industry.
[4] *Town and Country Planning*, vol. 15, 1947.
[5] *The Plan that Pleased.*
[6] *Town and Country Planning*, 1948.
[7] Mechanical Engineering Research Laboratory of the Department of Scientific and Industrial Research UK.
[8] *The Plan that Pleased.*
[9] *Town and Country Planning*, June 1951.
[10] *Town and Country Planning*, 1951.
[11] *Town and Country Planning*, vol. 19, 1951.
[12] *Town and Country Planning*, 1952.
[13] Ibid.
[14] Ibid.
[15] *Town and Country Planning*, 1953.
[16] *Town and Country Planning*, 1952.
[17] Ibid.
[18] *The Plan that Pleased.*
[19] Ibid.
[20] *Hamilton Advertiser*, March 1954.
[21] *The Plan that Pleased.*
[22] Ibid.
[23] Ibid.
[24] Ibid.
[25] *Town and Country Planning*, 1953.

[27] *The Plan that Pleased*, p.45.
[28] *The Plan that Pleased*.
[29] *The Plan that Pleased*.
[30] *Town and Country Planning*, vol. 23, 1955.
[31] *Town and Country Planning*, vol. 24, 1956.
[32] *Town and Country Planning*, October 1957.
[33] Ibid.
[34] *Town and Country Planning*, vol. 27, 1959.
[35] Ibid.
[36] *Town and Country Planning*, vol. 26, 1958.
[37] *Town and Country Planning*, vol. 27, 1959.
[38] Verbal information from Sir Robert.

Chapter 8

Retirement to Stirling 1963-1980

In 1962 Miss Elizabeth's elder sister, Marian, died and left her house, 19 Clarendon Place, Stirling to Miss Elizabeth. This seemed a good moment for the three remaining sisters to move from Langlees. The house was a big one. Driving was becoming more difficult as the sisters grew older and the road into Biggar could be very icy in the winter though Miss Elizabeth had been known to walk it even in snowy weather. Staff was becoming increasingly difficult to get. In 1964 Miss Margaret and Miss Veronica moved into the town to a bungalow, then called East Park, south of Biggar High Street overlooking the golf course.

As part of the move from Langlees Miss Elizabeth organised the disposal of family belongings collected over almost fifty years. It was at this time that she came to St. George's School with clothes for the acting cupboard. Though she was by then over eighty she came under her own steam, there was no sign of a taxi, and she refused politely but firmly to let the Headmistress take her to her next destination.

When she first moved to Stirling Miss Mitchell seems to have had a fairly interesting social life. In the summer of 1967 she was delighted when 'great tall Andrew' (Monteath) appeared at her door. 'Such a grand officer', she wrote later to his mother, adding sadly that he was already older than her brother Andrew had ever been.[1] She had many other visitors. Among the nearest relations were her third cousin Robert and his wife Frances Mitchell who lived at Dunblane. At first the visits were rather difficult for Miss Elizabeth had the reputation in the family of being a blue stocking, but soon the shyness wore off. Their daughter, Matilda, who was working at Stirling University, also became a friend and admirer. With Matilda Miss Mitchell drove round the local wooded countryside round Stirling. She noted that what used to be woodland was now under the plough and that what had been ploughed fields was now covered with dense softwood plantations. Bell

81

Miss Mitchell with her sisters Margaret and Veronica
by kind permission of Biggar Museum

Macfarlane Gay and his wife were also visitors at Clarendon Place and their children played in Miss Elizabeth's garden. Among her other visitors were W.A.P. Jack, the architect, the Provost of Stirling and the Chairman of the University Appeal. Very regular visitors were the Rev. J. Warnock and his wife. Sometimes they brought with them Kate McMinn who for nearly fifty years had been the housekeeper at Langlees. In 1974 Miss Mitchell noted that Kate had spent four or five weeks at Langlees while the new occupants, the Clydesmuirs, were in China. Miss Mitchell thought that Kate might have frightened away a burglar who thought that the house was empty. When she had left Langlees Kate had been promised a council house on one floor because by that time she had an arthritic hip and was very lame. For a time she went to the Law hospital for physiotherapy and eventually she was called in to have an operation on her hip. A relation who visited her the day after she was admitted found her cheerful, but the next day she died under the operation. She was only sixty-seven.[2]

In 1967 Miss Mitchell visited the new towns of Glenrothes and Livingston and wrote an article: 'Twenty One Years Tale' telling the history of the towns since the New Town Act.[3] In 1970 she had a very happy day in Glasgow when she met some of her 'old pals' in the Town and Country Planning Association and heard Lord Wheatly talk about his Committee's Report. The talk she found interesting but she was very doubtful about plans to include Glasgow in the new Western Region.[4]

She sometimes came to Edinburgh to see her friends. In 1973 she stayed at the Ladies' Caledonian Club in Charlotte Square and found her way to the new St James's Centre which she said gave her the 'jim jams'. She managed to find her way into the shopping centre but had great difficulty finding her way out. When she did get out she found herself in the bus station among the buses. She did not think that the new buildings fitted well into Georgian Edinburgh and wondered who had been the architect and planner.[5]

During this same visit she went again to St George's School and was delighted to see how well the buildings and grounds had settled. She recalled in a letter to a friend that the then Headmistress, Miss Stevenson, the Chairman of the Governors, Lord Salveson, and herself had been the people responsible for planning the grounds instead of the desolate market garden which had previously occupied the top of the hill.[6]

Even after she had moved to Stirling Miss Mitchell often came back to Biggar to see her sisters. In 1969 Miss Margaret died quite suddenly and in 1974 Miss Veronica died after a few weeks of illness. The Rev. J. Warnock remembered that Miss Elizabeth faced these bereavements with courage and serenity based on profound faith. Dr Marshall, who had attended Miss Veronica, was told by Miss Elizabeth that he must buy her sisters' house. She even told him how much to offer, and the property was his in a matter of days. He thought that Miss Elizabeth had wanted him to buy the house because she had planted a hedge and wanted someone who would take proper care of it.[7] Miss Elizabeth noted with satisfaction that she had known him since he was 'a little inquiring toddler' and she added with satisfaction that he was a good gardener.[8] It is said that the medals of Miss Margaret's fiancé, who had been killed in the 1914-18 war, were buried under the lawn of the bungalow.[9]

In 1971 the Rev. J. Warnock celebrated twenty-five years in the parish and Miss Mitchell came to the celebrations.

Characteristically, Miss Mitchell saw where she could be helpful and took action dividing 19 Clarendon Place into two parts, creating a flat which could be rented to staff of the new university. This sort of accommodation was very welcome to the university in a town which was unaccustomed to university housing needs.

In Stirling Miss Elizabeth was looked after by Mysie Marnoch, a very devoted maid about twenty years younger than herself.

In December 1974 she complained that she was feeling her age but admitted that at 94 'it is not surprising to feel a little decayed'. She was still vividly interested in current affairs and wished that there was someone like Churchill to rally the nation. She thought Whitelaw old and probably tired. She certainly did not think Wilson or Heath could do the job and she did not see any women about to play Jeanne d'Arc. A year later she reported that she had been in bed with 'a tiresome though not deadly complaint, lumbago' and that though she was improving she was not yet allowed out of the house. In November 1975, having had the experience of tidying up the belongings of her sisters, Miss Mitchell began to think of disposing of her books and approached the Librarian of Stirling University. First she offered him a well preserved calf-bound set of Gibbon's *Decline and Fall* but the University had a copy. Then on 3 April 1976 Miss Mitchell wrote to the Librarian to ask if he, or one of his staff, could come and look at what she had to offer. The Librarian was grateful for a 2-volume edition of *Tom Jones* and a second edition of *The Provost*. The University chose thirty books:

Yeats' Poems (1912)

Carlyle, *Sartor Resartus* (1841)

Bagehot, *Literary Studies*, edited by R.H. Hunter (1873, 1879)

John Buchan, *Grey Weather* (1899)

James Barrie, *A Window in Thrums* (1892)

Samuel Johnson, *Prayers and Meditations*; preface by A. Burrell (no date),

Hawthorne *Tales* (no date)

Mrs Wyndham Knight Bruce, *The Story of an African Chief* (1893)

James Hogg, *The poems of James Hogg*, edited by W. Wallace (1903)

Ian Lindsay, *Georgian Edinburgh* (1948)

Wordsworth, *The Prelude*, edited by E. de Selincourt (1942)

Tennyson, *Maud and other poems* (1874)

Tennyson, *Poems* (1868)

Synge, *Plays, Poems and Prose* (1946)

R.L. Stevenson, *Some Letters* compiled by L. Osborne (1917)

Eric Stair-Kerr, *Stirling Castle and its place in Scottish Heritage* (1913)

Avril Stewart, *The Links of Clyde* (1941)

Kuno Mayer, *Selections from Ancient Poetry* (1928)

W.M. Macgregor, *Christ and Church* (1937)

R. Simpson, *Traditions of the Covenanters* (no date)

A.E. Popham, *Raphael & Michelangelo* (1954)

John Morley, *Life of Gladstone* (abridged, no date)

M. Hurlemann, *The Mediterranean*, translated by E.D. Becul (1937)

M. Hurlemann, *Ewiges Griechenland* (1944)

G. Vasari, *Lives of the most eminent painters, sculptors and architects* (1897)

Froissart, *Chronicles* (1839)

Lecky, *History of European morals* (1869)

Titian's Paintings and drawings (1937)

C. Doughty, *Travels in the Arctic* (1926)

E.B. Mitchell, *The Plan that Pleased* (1967)

It is an interesting collection and shows how Miss Mitchell was buying books into the 30s and 40s and that most of these were poetry or art or history. When she died her Executors offered all her books to Stirling University and the Librarian sent round a van. The University offered £50 for the books but the Executors explained that they were sure Miss Mitchell would have wanted them to be a gift.

Mitchell Family tombstone, Dean Cemetery. Edinburgh
taken by Antonia Reeve

In March 1977 she had a stroke and as she put it herself in a Christmas letter, 'everybody thought that was the end of Miss M but lo! after a fortnight unconscious I came to life again, at a lower level but not bad for 97.' Her faithful Mysie, aged 73, was still able to take charge and they managed to find a very competent helper who came twice a week. She had various friends and neighbours who visited her, among them W.A.P. Jack and Mrs Muriel Macfarlane Grey, and, of course, The Rev. J. and Mrs Warnock.

Then she developed breast cancer and on the morning of her 100th birthday she died very peacefully. The old girls of St. George's had sent her flowers and relations had sent telegrams. Mysie was looking after her. Her publishers had hoped to send her a reprint of her book on Canada as a birthday present but she never knew.

A funeral service was held at Warriston Crematorium where the small chapel was full to overflowing. Representatives of Miss Mitchell's various interests were much in evidence. There was an excellent oration by the Rev. J. Warnock which Matilda, who had taken a day off to attend, remembered a decade later. Some considerable time later Mr Warnock was invited to meet some members of the family at Miss Mitchell's house in Stirling. From there they proceeded to the Dean Cemetery in Edinburgh where he conducted a short service, and a small casket with Miss Mitchell's ashes was buried in the family grave. Her name had already been engraved on the headstone.

By 1991 the headstone had cracked into two pieces near the top and these were lying behind the rest of the tombstone which was the part with the names and dates of all the Mitchell family, from Helen who had died in 1892 to Miss Elizabeth who died in 1980. The headstone has now been mended.

When she died, Miss Elizabeth left £750 to the Town and Country Planning Association and £2,500 to East Kilbride. The two sums have been put together and are now used to encourage children of East Kilbride to take an interest in their environment. She had already made various anonymous gifts to Biggar, and her old school had a Mitchell Bursary.

[1] Miss Mitchell to Mrs Monteath 14 December 1967.
[2] Verbal information from the Rev. J. Warnock.
[3] Miss Mitchell to Mrs Monteath 14 December 1967.
[4] Miss Mitchell to Mrs Monteath 22 January 1970.
[5] Miss Mitchell to Mrs Monteath 9 June 1973.
[6] Miss Mitchell to Mrs Monteath 9 June 1973.
[7] Verbal information from Dr Marshall.
[8] Letter from Miss Mitchell to Mrs Monteath 20 December 1974.
[9] Information from Rev. J. Warnock.

Chapter 9

Miss E.B. Mitchell as a person

What was Miss Elizabeth like as a person? The character that emerges from *The Plan that Pleased, Canada before the War* and the files of *Town and Country Planning* is of someone with a great zest for life, whether it involved getting to know women in rural Saskatchewan or learning to understand the intricacies of town planning legislation and local government administration. Whatever she did she did with her whole heart and she enjoyed. She was modest and quite prepared to be Hon. Secretary and let someone else be Chairman. She had no interest in asserting her own importance. Her contributions to the magazine *Town and Country Planning* reveal some more characteristics. She was quite incapable of using a cliché. She thought honestly, clearly and perceptively and she wrote clear, lively, perceptive reports. Sometimes she revealed a mischievious sense of humour. She had an unerring capacity for putting her finger on the essential point. She had a down to earth understanding of the people who lived in her new town whether they were women who wanted local shops or safe road crossings for toddlers and homes with a front door from the street or little boys who needed a shed in the back yard where they could make things. She never laughed at them. They were her friends. One example of this instinctive interest in people was when she heard that the Biggar minister had close ties with East Kilbride. His mother had been born, brought up and married from a farm there and her sister and brothers had taken over another farm, Newhousemill, on the Torrance estate which was designated to become part of the new town. When Mr Warnock went to Biggar in 1946 one of his uncles was still in Newhousemill Farm.

Miss Elizabeth got to know the farmer and learnt a great deal about the Torrance estate on which he was the oldest surviving tenant. She made good use of his knowledge when she was planning the planting. The farmer died in 1954 but years afterwards in 1968, when a new church was built where his farm had stood, Newhousemill/Claremont Church, arrangements were made for the Rev. J. Warnock and his wife to be present at the dedication.

Mr Warnock, who knew her well for thirty-four years, thought of her as a 'coalescence of contradiction'. She was a visionary yet very practical. She could appear remote, aloof, alone and yet was kind, sincere and genial. She could be tough on a Town Council or any other meeting but was also very tender. In public she was fearless and intrepid but she was personally self-effacing and even shy. She could be a confident, dignified public figure but was personally a very private person. Though she had high academic achievements she would take immense pains over the very dull details of planning. She had no interest in changing fashions and was perfectly happy to attend a Church meeting in an old coat, hat, and scarf and boots and she always had an umbrella or a stick. She was deeply religious but never made any parade of this. In her, conviction led to dedication and an unrelenting passionate campaign of active service.

She could be concise and incisive but never strident. People who had worked with her spoke of her charm and sincerity. These qualities showed in her capacity to relate to children whether they were Glasgow evacuees, the children of friends or her god-daughter who came to tea at Langlees. She would provide something that they would like to do. She never forced them to do something she thought they ought to enjoy. At the end of the visit the children would find that they had learned a great deal about wild flowers or local history without realising it.

The text on the family tombstone in Dean Cemetery on the Queensferry Road, Edinburgh expresses her religion perfectly. It is from Micah, chapter 6, verse 8: 'What doth the Lord require of thee, but to do justly, and to love mercy, and to walk humbly with thy God?'

As one reads her writing fragments of a biblical quotation keep coming into one's head and gradually one recognises the 13th chapter of St. Paul's 1st Epistle to the Corinthians.

Charity suffereth long and is kind; charity envieth not; charity vaunteth not itself; is not puffed up; doth not behave itself unseemly, seeketh not her own, is not easily provoked, thinketh no evil; rejoiceth not in iniquity, but rejoiceth in the truth; beareth all things, believeth all things, hopeth all things, endureth all things.

It is a very good picture of Miss Elizabeth Buchanan Mitchell.

Appendix 1

Divisions within the Church of Scotland

The Church of Scotland was established by law as the national church in 1560, and after over a century of religious and civil war was re-established by Act of Parliament in 1690 but already there had been one schism and a group calling themselves **Cameronians** after their founder and popularly ' known as the Covenantors had split off because they would not accept a king who did not subscribe to the Covenant.

In the eighteenth century two more groups broke off from the established church. In 1732 Ebenezer Erskine refused to accept a decision by the General Assembly of the Church of Scotland that in cases where the patron, under the Act of 1712 restoring lay patronage, neglected or declined to exercise his right the new minister might be chosen by the Elders and the Protestant heritors, or landowners, but that the rest of the congregation would have no share in the appointment. In 1733 he was joined by some other Presbyterians who called themselves the **Associate Presbytery**.

In 1761 Thomas Gillespie, Minister of Carrick, was deposed by the General Assembly because he refused to take part in the ordination of a candidate who was not acceptable to his congregation. Gillespie continued to minister to his people in a field. This he did for fifteen years; then he was joined by two other ministers, one of them an English dissenter. They founded a presbytery 'for the Relief of Christians oppressed in their Christian principles'. This came to be known as the **Relief Church**.

In 1747 the Associated Presbytery had split into two sections, the **Burghers** and the **Antiburghers**. The Burghers considered that it was acceptable for their members to take the oath of loyalty required of all burghers 'to uphold the true religion as by law established'.

The Antiburghers refused to take this oath. Miss Mitchell's great great grandfather was an Anti-burgher.

Later in the eighteenth century the Burghers and Antiburghers split again

91

into groups known as the **Auld Lichts** and the **New Lichts**. This was over the extent to which the church was prepared to rely on the civil power to punish religious errors. The New Lichts did not accept this view.

In 1820 the New Licht Burghers and Antiburghers joined to form what was called the **United Secession Church**. The Auld Licht Burghers in 1839 joined the Church of Scotland. The Auld Licht Antiburghers continued their independent existence for the time being.

In 1841 part of the United Secession Church became the **Evangelical Union** which eventually joined the Congregational Church.

In 1847 the bulk of the United Secession Church joined the Relief church to become the **United Presbyterian** which was the part of the church that Miss Mitchell's great grandfather ministered to in the very splendid Wellington Church in Glasgow.

In 1843 came the Disruption when many of the ministers and brethren walked out of the General Assembly of the Church of Scotland and founded the **Free Church**.

Gradually the various different sections of the Church came together. In 1850 the majority of the Auld Licht Antiburghers joined the Free Church. In 1876 the Reformed Presbyterian Church which was the name of the Cameronians or Covenanters also joined the Free Church. In 1900 the United Presbyterians joined the Free Church when they both took the name of the **United Free Church**. The majority of this group in 1929 rejoined the Church of Scotland.

The Evangelical Union branch of the Secession Church joined the Congregational Church.

The divisions can best be understood from the diagram opposite.

Church of Scotland as by law established 1560 and again 1690

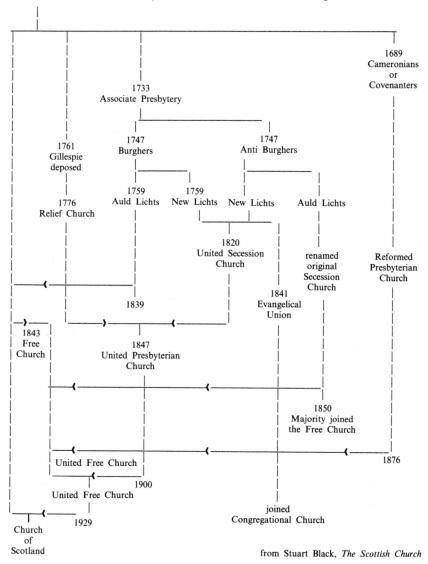

from Stuart Black, *The Scottish Church*

94   *Elizabeth B. Mitchell*

Appendix 2

The Mitchell Family Tree much simplified

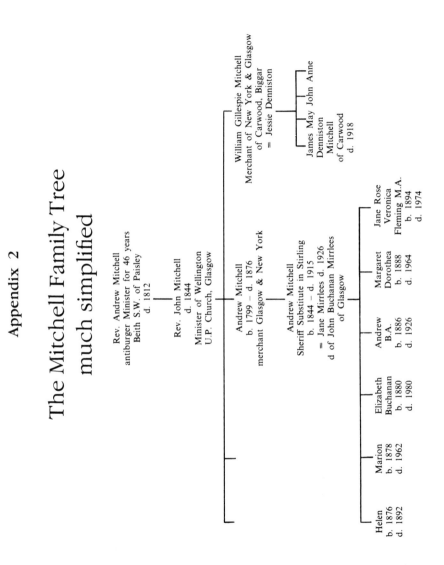

Rev. Andrew Mitchell
antiburger Minister for 46 years
Beith S.W. of Paisley
d. 1812

Rev. John Mitchell
d. 1844
Minister of Wellington
U.P. Church, Glasgow

Andrew Mitchell
b. 1799 – d. 1876
merchant Glasgow & New York

William Gillespie Mitchell
Merchant of New York & Glasgow
of Carwood, Biggar
= Jessie Denniston

James May John Anne
Denniston
Mitchell
of Carwood
d. 1918

Andrew Mitchell
Sheriff Substitute in Stirling
b. 1844 – d. 1915
= Jane Mirrlees d. 1926
d of John Buchanan Mirrlees
of Glasgow

Helen
b. 1876
d. 1892

Marion
b. 1878
d. 1962

Elizabeth
Buchanan
b. 1880
d. 1980

Andrew
B.A.
b. 1886
d. 1926

Margaret
Dorothea
b. 1888
d. 1964

Jane Rose
Veronica
Fleming M.A.
b. 1894
d. 1974

The Rev Andrew Mitchell, the second minister of Beith church, was inducted in 1765. About the seventeenth year of his ministry the Beith congregation became involved in bitter hostility over the Lifter controversy. This had originated in Ayrshire. Those who supported the Lifter side insisted that it was right in the Communion Service to lift the bread and the wine before the prayer of consecration. Dr John Mitchell, son of the Rev. Andrew remembered the Leader of the Beith Lifters haranguing the people with the foam flying from his lips, and urging his hearers to stand fast in their belief or they would rot in their graves. The Rev. Andrew was a man of forebearing character and stood fast in spite of the very bitter and hostile attacks. He remained the minister for forty-six years.[1]

The Rev. John Mitchell, son of the Rev. Andrew, was the first Minister of Wellington Church in Glasgow. The church had been founded in 1792 for an overflow from Duke Street – the Mother Antiburgher church of Glasgow. The Rev. John Mitchell was called to the ministry in 1793 at which time his stipend was £80 a year. In 1807 he was made a D.D. by Princeton College, New Jersey and in 1837 by Glasgow University, by which time his stipend had risen to £300 and he had been chosen by the Synod to be Professor of Bibilical History.[2]

Miss Elizabeth said that all her four grandparents had been born in Glasgow and certainly her Mitchell grandfather was a Glasgow merchant, though he had connections with New York where her own father was born.

Her mother's family, the Mirrlees, are commemorated by Mirrlees Drive and Mirrlees Lane in the Gowanhill area of West Glasgow and the names indicate the family's estate in the residential area near the Botanic Gardens. They had lived in Redlands House which is commemorated by Redlands Terrace to the north of the Great West Road west of the Botanic Gardens. It was from this house that Miss Mitchell's mother was married in 1875.

Of the rest of the family, Helen died as a schoolgirl of measles. Andrew, having been educated at the Edinburgh Academy, went on to Pembroke College, Cambridge where he studied Engineering, graduating in 1908. He worked first with Messrs James Howden for six months and then with John Cowan for another six months; from 1911–14 he worked for Messrs Cowan and Wilson. In 1914 Mr Cowan proposed him for Associate membership of the Institute of Civil Engineers. One of his seconders was Mr Wilson and another Mr Cowan. In all he had seven seconders among whom was W.J. Mirrlees. The second daughter, Marion, settled in Stirling after her father died, and eventually left her house to Miss Elizabeth. The fourth daughter, Margaret, did a good deal of voluntary work, especially for the Women's

Guild of the Church in Biggar and Queensberry House, in which she took a great interest. The youngest sister, Veronica, went to Lady Margaret Hall in 1913 and read Modern History in which she got a second class. After leaving the University she worked in the Ministry of Labour as a clerk, then for the League of Nations Union and after 1929 in the Women's Guild of the Church of Scotland.

[1] R. Small, *History of the Congregations of the U.P. Church 1733-1900*.
[2] Ibid.

Bibliography

Georgina Battiscombe, *Reluctant Pioneer* (Constable, 1978)

W. Hunter, *Biggar and the House of Fleming* (William Paterson, Edinburgh, 1860; 2nd Ed. 1867)

David Littlejohn, *Biggar Town Trail* (compiled while a pupil at Biggar High School 1981; Revised 1990)

Moray McLaren, *Shell Guide to Scotland* (Ebury Press, 1965)

E.B. Mitchell, *Canada before the War* (Murray, London, 1915)

E.B. Mitchell, *The Plan that Pleased* (Town and Country Planning Association, London, 1967)

E.B. Mitchell, *Agriculture in Scotland Today and Tomorrow* (pamphlet for Church discussion groups, United Free Church of Scotland, Edinburgh on behalf of their Federation of Young People's Societies, 1921)

Lady Winifred Peck, *A Little Learning* (Faber, 1952)

R. Small, *History of the Congregations of the U.P. Church 1733-1900* (David M. Small, Edinburgh, 1904)

Obituary of Andrew Mitchell, *Scots Law Times* 29 May 1915

Ordnance Gazeteer of Scotland 1882–5 (Jack, Edinburgh)

St. George's Chronicle (published by the school since 1894)

St. George's Jubilee Chronicle (published by the school, 1938)

Statistical Account 1791–99 (published in sections from 1792 onwards by W. Creech)

New Statistical Account (Blackwood, 1845)

3rd Statistical Account (Oliver & Boyd, 1952)

Town and Country Planning (Town and Country Planning Association) Periodical sometimes quarterly, sometimes monthly

Report of the Committee on Women in Agriculture in Scotland (HMSO, 1920)

UNPRINTED MATERIAL

St. George's School Council Minutes vol. 2 (14 February 1924 – February 1954). Refers to previous meetings but no minutes extant.
St. George's School Committee Minutes vol. 2 (January 1923 – July 1949)
St. George's College Minutes
St. George's General Meetings
St. George's Finance Committee Minutes
  (All the surviving minutes of St. George's School are deposited with Chiene & Tait, 3 Albyn Place, Edinburgh)
Birth Certificate: Miss E.B. Mitchell, Register House
Death Certificate: Andrew Mitchell, Register House
Family tree in possession of Mrs Matilda Hall, née Mitchell
Minutes of the Lanarkshire Education Committee (Mitchell Library, Glasgow)